According to one Tennessee hillsman speaking in 1933, Roosevelt's New Deal consisted of "a President in a white shirt and a gang of nosy revenuers." It was the hillsman's opinion that "them guvment fellers are a little crazy."

The Tennessean was talking about the TVA (the Tennessee Valley Authority) which was created in 1933 to save a region that had been depressed for a century, long before anyone had heard of the great depression of '29. But now, with the New Deal, everyone—cantankerous hill folk, sharecroppers, and "them guvment fellers"—came together to try to change things, in one of the greatest regional planning experiments ever devised. Soon over twenty great dams and their powerhouses were built to harness the river. Farmers diverted their wornout fields from cotton to clover. Electric lights went on for the first time, and for the first time there was radio in the parlor—Fibber McGee and Molly, Jack Benny.

The Living History Library, under the general editorship of John Anthony Scott, is a new series that provides a fresh, challenging, and human approach to the study of America's past. Its overall theme as a series is the history of the United States as told by the people who shaped it.

VALLEY OF VISION

The Living History Library

General editor: John Anthony Scott

VALLEY OF VISION

THE TVA YEARS

Martha E. Munzer

Illustrated with contemporary prints, photographs, & maps

ALFRED A. KNOPF : NEW YORK

*This book was written under the auspices
of the Conservation Foundation.*

CONTENTS

VALLEY OF VISION

☆ | 1 | ☆

A GREAT NATURAL FABRIC

This is the story of a huge twentieth-century rescue operation—the harnessing of the turbulent Tennessee River and the revitalizing of the land through which it flows. It is also the story of a great river valley, a valley that stretches across seven states and contains over 40,000 square miles of Southern land—an area larger than England and Scotland combined. Above all, it is the story of the rebirth of hope in people whose lives and well-being are inseparably linked with the changing fortunes of their river and their valley home.

But before the twentieth-century drama can unfold, the stage must be set in the past, where it all began.

Dwelling in the Tennessee valley some 200 years ago were tribes of Cherokee, Creek, Choctaw, and Chickasaw Indians. They believed they were part of a great natural fabric which they could not harm without injury and even grave danger to themselves. An eighteenth-century writer gave a vivid picture of their attitude:

To the Indian there were spirits everywhere and all natural forces were either spirits or the expression of spirits.

Sacrifice was generally in the nature of a gift to the spirits that especially affected human welfare. Beautiful beads, amulets, ornaments, feathered articles and embroideries in porcupine quills, were frequently offered to the spirits of the springs, the fishing places, the cornfields or in the woods where flocks of game birds had been killed.

Where some animal, such as the bear, had been killed, the Indian knelt down beside it and built a little ceremonial fire upon which he cast a tobacco incense. He would address the spirit of the bear, seeking to curb its anger at having been slain. "O brother bear, do not be angry," the Indian would say, "I needed your skin and your flesh, for I must have clothing and meat to eat. The Great Spirit has made both of us, but he has made man more cunning. I have not slain you for malice or for mere sport, so be not angry. I should not have been angry had you slain me. Come accept my sacrifice. See I cast aside the arrow that killed you. Watch it burn. See I give you these beads and this knife, accept them as my gift to you and invoke no harm to me."

The Spaniards came and went, leaving the Indians and their way of life and their countryside comparatively undisturbed. As English traders and explorers gradually pushed westward from the settlements on the seaboard and Frenchmen pressed eastward from the Mississippi, they saw the beauty of the springs, cornfields, and woods of the Indian's world. Botanist William Bartram, who journeyed to the land of the Cherokee on the headwaters of the Little Tennessee River, described the mountainous southeastern part of the valley in his *Travels*, in 1777:

After riding near two miles through Indian plantations of Corn, which was well cultivated, kept clean of weeds and was well advanced, being near eighteen inches in height, and the Beans planted at the Corn-hills were above ground, we leave the fields on our right, turning towards the mountains and ascending through a delightful green vale or lawn, which conducted us in amongst the pyramidal hills and crossing a brisk flowing creek, meandering through the meads which continued near two miles, dividing and branching in amongst the hills; we then mounted their steep ascents, rising gradually by ridges or steps one above another, frequently crossing narrow, fertile dales as we ascended; the air feels cool and animating . . .

Bartram's party reached a high ridge, and then

We began to descend the mountain on the other side, which exhibited the same order of gradations of ridges and vales as on our ascent; and at length rested on a very expansive, fertile plain, amidst the towering hills, over which we rode a long time, through magnificent high forest, extensive green fields, meadows and lawns . . . We came to a fine little river, which crossing, and riding over fruitful strawberry beds and green lawns, on the sides of a circular ridge of hills in front of us, and going round the bases of this promontory, came to a fine meadow on an arm of the vale, through which meandered a brook, its humid vapours bedewing the *fragrant strawberries which hung in heavy red clusters over the grassy verge . . .*

Overall, the valley of Bartram's travels was as irregular, as various, as rebellious as the great Tennessee River, which drained it. In the east, fluted lands, a succession of fertile valleys and ridges. At its center, terracelands and rich lowlands. In the west, bottomlands. The hills had mineral wealth—soft coal and iron ore, marble and zinc. There was fertile soil, a forest cover of tall, sturdy timber—pine, oak, and hickory—and a beneficent climate. Branching through this luxuriant wilderness were myriad streams that emptied into the turbulent Tennessee.

By the late 1700s, glowing accounts of this rich land beyond the Appalachian Mountains were coming back to the settlers on the eastern seaboard. A few of the most adventuresome now pushed westward. Starting in the 1770s came Scots, Irish, English, Germans, Dutch, and a sprinkling of French Huguenots. Some struggled through the Appalachian mountain gaps, but most trekked through the great Appalachian valley, from Pennsylvania, from Maryland, and from Virginia. A few braved the danger-fraught Tennessee River in flatboats.

But the Tennessee was a dangerous river to travel. There were shoals and sandbars, swift currents, and seasons of low water. Muscle Shoals, in the Great Bend of the river, was one of the most famous and treacherous spots. After the shoals came Widow's Bar, and beyond that, for a distance of about twenty miles, was a turbulent section called by the first boatmen and travelers the Narrows. It was pronounced "Narrs" by the pioneers. The Frying Pan, the Boiling Pot, the Suck, and Tumbling Shoals were among the fanciful names that pioneer boatmen applied to various sections of the Narrows.

Before recounting the history of the great 650-mile waterway as told by its travelers, let us take a close look at its course as depicted on a map of today.

From the spot where the Holston and French Broad Rivers meet and mingle, in the Appalachian Mountain valley between the Cumberland Range and the Great Smoky Mountains, the Tennessee River starts its journey, flowing in a southwest direction across the eastern part of Tennessee. Then it turns westward just below Chattanooga at Walden Gorge; from there it flows southwestward into Alabama, then westward again across the northern part of the state to the tip of northeastern Mississippi. The arc thus described by the river has been known from Indian times as the Great Bend. Beyond this arc, the Tennessee flows almost due north through the western section of Tennessee and Kentucky. Finally, the river joins the Ohio at what is now the city of Paducah, Kentucky. The Ohio, in turn, empties into the Mississippi, which finds its outlet in the Gulf of Mexico at New Orleans.

Perhaps the most famous party of hopeful farmers to travel the Tennessee via flatboat was John Donelson's fleet of 30 boats and dugout canoes, with 200 people, in 1779–1780. Their flatboats—variously called broadhorns, Kentucky boats, and arks—were to be knocked apart at the end of the journey and the lumber used to erect cabins.

Here is part of the story of the Donelson party's attempt to navigate the turbulent river:

December 22, 1779. Took our departure from the fort and fell down to the mouth of Reedy creek, where we were stopped by the fall of water and most excessive hard frost . . .

February 27, 1780. Struck the Poor-valley shoals, on which shoal we lay that afternoon and succeeding night in much distress.

Monday, February 28, 1780. In the morning, the water rising, we got off the shoal, after landing thirty persons to lighten our boat. In attempting to land on an island, received some damage, and lost sundry articles, and came to camp on the south shore, where we joined sundry other vessels also bound down . . .

By March 9, the fleet had arrived at the Whirl, or Suck, "where the river is compressed within less than half of its common width above, by the Cumberland Mountains, which jut in on both sides." They passed through the upper part of these Narrows at the Boiling Pot. Then, on Sunday, March 12, the company reached notorious Muscle Shoals.

After trimming our boats in the best manner possible, we ran through the shoals before night. When we approached them they had a dreadful appearance to those who had never seen them before. The water being high made a terrible roaring, which could be heard at some distance among the driftwood heaped frightfully upon the points of the island, the current running in every

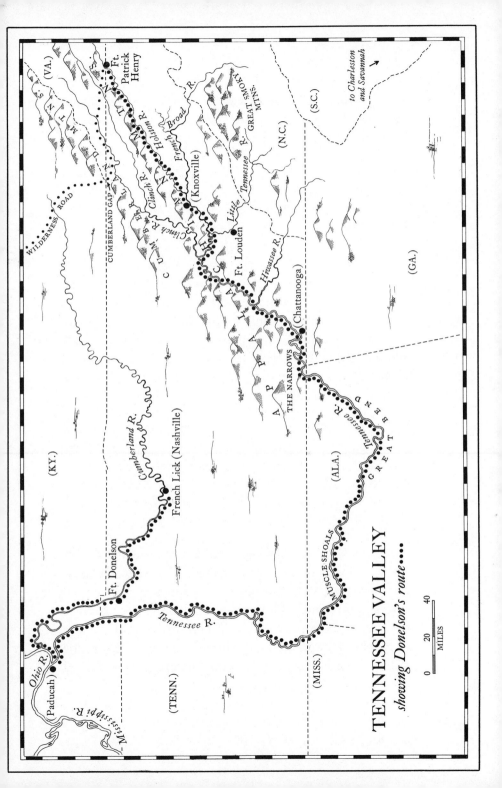

TENNESSEE VALLEY
showing Donelson's route••••

possible direction. Here we did not know how soon we should be dashed to pieces, and all our troubles ended at once.

After many adventures and misadventures, including bloodcurdling encounters with Indians, the Donelson party finally reached its destination on the Cumberland River on April 24, 1780: "This day we arrived at our journey's end at the Big Salt Lick. Though our prospects at present are dreary, we have found a few log-cabins which have been built on a cedar bluff above the Lick by Capt. Robertson and his company."

This was the beginning. Soon the push to the southwest gained enormous impetus. Newspaper articles advertised the sale of the rich unopened valley land and proposed settling expeditions. A typical article appeared in 1788 in the Kentucky *Gazette:*

The soil is fertile as Kentucky, the climate infinitely more agreeable, better calculated for raising cotton, indigo and the different productions of the climate. Its situation is perhaps as convenient as any on the western waters lying on the navigable and beautiful river Tenese, which affords an infinite variety of fine fish, etc.

So the first clearings began to be made in the forests and the first crude cabins erected. For the settlers it was a rugged life, fostering independence and an insistent self-reliance. Quite understandably, get-togethers were all-important events. Wherever possible, there would be a "working"—sorghum making, quilting, log rolling, corn hoeing, corn husking, or house raising. And

"Burning Trees—Spring":
this lithograph is from the original painting
by George Harvey.

when the work was done, there were songs and singing games—English, Scottish, and Irish—brought over from the Old Country.

A British ballad called "Berkshire Tragedy" became in its American version "The Knoxville Girl"—for already Knoxville was a fast-growing settlement.

The Knoxville Girl

I fell in love with a Knoxville girl
With dark and rolling eyes,
I promised her I'd marry her
If me she'd ne'er deny.

I called her at her sister's house,
About nine o'clock at night,
And little did that fair girl think
I owned her in a fright.

I said to her, "Let's take a walk
And view the meadows gay
That we might have a little talk
And plan our wedding day."

We walked along, we talked along,
Till we came to level ground.
There I picked up an edgewood stick
And I knocked that fair girl down.

After the singing might come a "frolic" to the tune of a fiddle. The fun would go on until the early hours.

Another kind of a get-together was the camp meeting. The three religious faiths in the valley were Presbyterian, Baptist, and Methodist, and in 1800 the South was swept by a great religious revival that spread like wildfire. To the first meeting, during which "many souls were saved," came one man who did not have enough horses for all his family to ride back and forth. So he stocked his wagon with provisions and they all camped out. Here was born the camp meeting: It was a revival service at which you camped out.

The meetings usually lasted for days. Scores of people were drawn together. Shouting was a feature from the first, and during the excitement, men and women would fall down in a trance. Others were seized by the "jerks." During the course of time some of this emotionalism would disappear, but in the main the people of the valley, especially those in the hills, clung to their other-worldly faith. Their own life on earth was hard, but would not God provide recompense in a future life? There was a note of resignation in this belief.

As the settlers attended camp meetings, cleared their land, and journeyed westward in ever-increasing numbers, the Indians were steadily pushed out of their wilderness—first came the cruel French and Indian War, then endless skirmishes between the remaining Stone Age peoples and the encroaching pioneers. It was an unequal contest. An Indian expert described the plight of the Cherokee, "Their fields and orchards wasted . . . their ammunition nearly exhausted, many of their bravest warriors dead, their people fugitives in the mountains, hiding in caves and living like beasts upon roots . . ." By 1838 the United States government had acted officially; it legislated the removal of the remaining Cherokee to the West. The great forced march, a brutal eviction, came to be known as the Trail of Tears.

And so by 1840, except for a small area in the hills where a handful of Indians remained hidden, the Tennessee valley, still for the most part a natural paradise, belonged to the white settlers. How would the newcomers use all these riches? After all, they brought with them a view of life entirely different from the Indian's. They had come to the New World firm in the belief that they had been granted God-given "dominion over the fish of the sea and over the fowl of the air, and over the cattle, and over all the earth, and over every creeping thing that creepeth upon the earth."

The settlers quickly found the soil in south-central Tennessee and northern Alabama ideal for raising cotton. Thoroughgoing farmers and planters brought their black slaves and gradually developed a prosperous agriculture. They grew cotton and tobacco, while on somewhat hillier land, many small farmers were busily raising sheep, hogs, and corn.

Tennessee's agriculture was flourishing in the 1840s and 1850s. These years were called the state's golden age of farming. In 1840 Tennessee raised more corn and more hogs than any other state. Her production of tobacco was topped only by Virginia, Kentucky, and Maryland. At an international exposition held in London in 1851, a middle Tennessee farmer won the medal for "the finest wool grown anywhere in the world" and a west Tennessee planter for the "best cotton known in the world."

Markets soon became necessary, especially for cotton, and the planters used the river to convey their crops to New Orleans. Keelboats replaced flatboats, and next came steamboats.

But the river was by nature wild, and it was ever a battle. In 1831, when the steamship *Knoxville* approached the Narrows, people flocked to the banks to watch the battle with the old river enemy—the Boiling Pot. A reporter wrote a blow-by-blow description of the fight, which lasted for a day and a half. On the morning of the second day:

About 12 o'clock, by the joint power of the steam and the capstan, the boat was seen in the middle of the stream, when the person whose business it was to unfasten the rope on shore, mistaking some cry on board for an order, cut the rope and left the boat to the stream and the current. For a moment she advanced—for another she hung trembling in a doubtful contest with the force of the water and began to recede. "Let go that anchor," cried the captain. "Ay, Ay, Sir," responded the mate, "Tis done." For the anchor to be cast, for a plank to be shoved over the guards—for several men to spring

*Keelboats were often used to carry
cotton to New Orleans.*

on the end of it to make it fast—for Barney Sedgewick, the mate, to leap from the end of it into the angry flood with a rope coiled around his neck and under his left arm—swim to shore, make it fast, and for the boat to be secure from impending ruin was the work of a moment. But it was a moment to the spectators of indescribable excitement . . .

The farmers would have to look for other routes to market, or soon improve the channel on their main waterway. For the Tennessee remained virtually cut in half by obstructions, while on the Mississippi and Ohio, steamboating was already in its heyday.

During these years various mineral resources also began to be discovered in the valley and soon attracted mining operations. Iron, lead, zinc, and other ores were abundant. There were coal deposits in the southern Appalachians, in Virginia, Kentucky, Tennessee, and Alabama. The mines brought quick wealth during their boom years.

The story of copper is typical. In the late 1840s prospectors discovered rich deposits of ore in a small southeastern section of Tennessee. Speculators and investors jumped to the chance, followed by a mass of humanity in search of a lucky strike.

> Out of the pines of Georgia
> From the laurel of Carolin'
> They came behind Buck and Bally,
> In search of the copper mine.
> They wielded their picks with ardor,
> They panned the streams up and down,

And out of their vision and labor
Was molded the famed Ducktown.

Ducktown, where this particular strike was made, was drawn into a hive of activity. One of the lucky promoters was John Caldwell, who described his windfall in a letter:

Ducktown, 1855

To Dr. R. O. Curry & C. A. Proctor
Gentlemen:
I came to Ducktown in 1849, scouting for copper and found some five or six tons in a cabin, 10 ft. square, on the property now known as the Hiwassee. I found the country unexplored . . . Sat down in the woods to mature some plan to open and control the section. I owned, at that time, one twenty dollar bill . . .
In May 1850, commenced mining in the woods. In the same year sunk two shafts, and obtained copper from both of them. The excavations made did not exceed twelve feet—at that depth the copper being found.

When such strikes ran out, the speculators were quick to locate others, and mine elsewhere.

Yes, the Tennessee valley was prospering; it was truly a golden age. But all this activity was stemmed by the increasingly bitter controversy over slavery.

The state of Tennessee itself was divided on the question, with eastern Tennessee and its small farmers tending to be antislavery. The rest of the state, especially the large plantation areas, was proslavery. In the end, the state threw in its lot with the Confederacy, along with the other states that extend into the valley: Virginia, North Carolina, Georgia, Alabama, Mississippi, and excluding only Kentucky.

Tennessee and Virginia were the two states where most of the fighting took place, and their lands were despoiled and devastated. The Tennessee valley itself became a wasteland from end to end after the battles of Chickamauga, Chattanooga, Knoxville, Franklin, and Nashville. Occupation by troops was constant. Homes, farms, and towns were completely ravaged.

One young soldier, John Wyeth, returned at the end of the war to his home in Guntersville, Alabama, in the Great Bend region of the Tennessee River. This was the scene he found:

> With the exception of half a dozen dwellings, which were spared because they shelter the sick and wounded . . . the village had disappeared. Nothing but tumbledown walls and a mass of brick debris was left of our home . . . We were not wholly unprepared for the scene of desolation about us. As we came west on the train nothing but lonesome-looking chimneys remained of the villages and farmhouses. They were suggestive of tombstones in a graveyard . . . Every town in northern Alabama . . . had been wiped out by the war policy of starvation by fire. Farmhouses, gins, fences, and cattle were gone. From a hilltop in the farming district a few miles from New Market I counted the chimneys of six different houses which had been destroyed.

Many Tennessee valley soldiers viewed similar scenes as they returned to what had once been their homes.

In the aftermath of war, the large, no-longer-operable plantations were quickly split up into small farms. Many returned soldiers, wiped out financially, had to become laborers on farms they had once owned. A poem in the *Southern Agriculturalist* lamented:

> *And twice a farm I've tried to buy*
> *But couldn't gather, low nor high,*
> *The cash I had to have in hand*
> *To get possession of the land.*
> *A slave to toil that has no end*
> *And does not help the lot to mend.*

As for the freed slaves, most who remained in the South became tenant farmers or sharecroppers, along with many poor whites wiped out by the war. Sharecropping and tenantry were the remnants of a master-slave system and permitted the survival of semislavery. Though both tenants and croppers rented from the landowner, the tenant usually supplied his own implements, mule, and seed. Not so the cropper, who lived in virtual serfdom. He was furnished the barest of supplies by the owner and was paid not in money, but with a small "share" of the crop, usually cotton. The percentage was so small that the cropper and his family after the war lived on a starvation diet and kept sinking deeper and deeper into debt.

Small farmers fortunate enough to own land were having their troubles too. The fields had been devastated by war, and the farmer needed every penny to keep himself and his family from going under. The best cash crops had always been corn, tobacco, and cotton, depending on the location. Now they were planted more than ever, even though these single crops grown year after year were beginning to rob the soil of its fertility. Observed one Tennessean at the time, "This [one-crop planting] is a most ruinous practice and tends greatly to impoverish the soil." And the State Agricultural Bureau warned that one-crop cultivation would lead to soil erosion which would doom Tennessee's agriculture.

But farmers simply could not afford to diversify now and continued to sow "row crops"—corn, cotton, or tobacco—in up- and down-hill rows. They even sowed the steep hillsides, to turn whatever acres they had to cash. As the plow went up and down the slopes, each groove became a kind of ditch. Rainwater surged down it, carrying off soil already exhausted of minerals by the monotonous crops.

To this incredible devastation of once fertile land was added the ravage of the forests. In the rebuilding of the South after the Civil War, lumber became the great moneymaker, lumber for burgeoning cities and fast-spreading railroads. The Tennessee valley was rich in forests—hardwood, yellow pine, cypress, and others. Some returned army officers set up small sawmills, but it was chiefly Northern capital that suddenly began investing in Southern timberland in large amounts. The scale was so grand and sawmilling so profitable that the business soon amounted to a slaughter. Once a forest was cut over, the investors hurried to another, or hurried back to the North with their profits. The era was a time of "cut out and get out."

Now, without its trees, the ground was no longer

protected by water-absorbing forest litter and humus. Live tree roots no longer held the earth in place. Rain-water tore away the topsoil, gouged out the slopes with deep gullies, and clogged the streams, often on the verge of overflowing anyway with mud and silt.

All this soil erosion enormously increased the likelihood of the floods to which the valley was subject. In winter, driving rainstorms swept through the mountains in the eastern part of the river valley. Folks had always expected high waters during February and March. They called it a "tide." But now the tide was more often an engulfing tidal wave.

The year 1867 furnished an unforgettable example. The very heavens seemed to open, pouring vast quantities of rain on soil that quickly became saturated. One rainstorm followed another steadily for two weeks. Lowlands along the entire basin of the Tennessee were flooded. Local newspapers carried the story.

Knoxville, March 6–8. We are now in the midst of a terrible flood. The waters are upon us and continue to come. The valuable bridge across the Holston has been swept away and not even a vestige can now be seen to indicate that such a structure even stood . . . The water stands at this time ten feet seven inches higher than known to the oldest inhabitant.

Wautauga, March 9. Homes, machinery, flatboats, laden with various products of the country, minus helmsmen or oarsmen, household and kitchen furniture, beds and clothing, etc., all these sailed along on the crest of the tide with great rapidity. A family, clinging to the wreck, crying aloud for assistance, but who, alas, were beyond the reach of human aid.

Chattanooga, March 10. The Tennessee River rose steadily at an average rate of four inches per hour, and to the driftwood and rafts floating upon its raging waters were added numerous log cabins and small dwelling houses that had been swept away from its bank . . . We have no heart this morning to dwell at length upon the terrible calamity which has befallen the citizens of Chattanooga and surrounding country. In Chattanooga, tonight, there is seven to eight feet of water on all the streets. The water was up to the base of the lime kiln on the cliff above the town. This shows that the water has risen fifty feet. It is stated that the backwater extends up Lookout Mountain Valley to a distance of forty miles from the river. A gentleman informs us that he has counted fifteen bodies of men, women and children, black and white, floating past his place on the road to Moccasin Bend.

Living out of range of the major floods, but in fact near the tributaries that were their source, were the hill people of Tennessee, Kentucky, and western Virginia. These were descendants of the first rugged settlers, and they were now completely out of touch with contemporary life. Sometimes fashionable writers in search of local color even sought them out as if they were romantic primitives. One wrote in *Atlantic Monthly* in 1889:

Is the lamp chimney lacking? The mountain potteries are still making flambeaux, lamps of almost classic pat-

A *sketch of corn husking that appeared*
in Atlantic Monthly, 1889, *with the caption,*
"I hear the laugh when the ear is red."

tern in which grease is burned with a floating wick. Is the sawmill remote? In the high mountains where streams are small and mills impracticable the whipsaw is brought into use, and two men will get out three or four hundred feet of boards from the logs in a day. Handmills for grinding can still be constructed by well-brought-up mountain men, and in some places they have not yet lost the tradition of the fashioning of the old English crossbow! And who does not have a feeling akin to reverence in the presence of a hand loom? When a mountain maid speaks of her "wheel" she does not refer to a bicycle, but to the spinning-wheel of our ancestors.

Actually, the life of the hill people was far from romantic. At the turn of the twentieth century, their highways were beds of streams; commerce and mail went by "horseflesh and saddlebags." The *Atlantic* writer asked the mountain woman if she ever went to town, fifteen miles away. " 'When you cannot get what you need at this little store down by the creek, where do you go?' The mountain woman answered with a frank smile, 'I go without.' And it appeared that she had never been to any town or city in her life."

She spoke for more than she knew. A century after white settlement of the valley, the people, the very earth itself, were going without. There were periodic floods. The soil had been depleted by war and by one-crop and row-crop farming. Forests had been slaughtered, and careless mining operations—running through vein after vein—had gored the land. How would these things affect the coming generations?

RAGGEDY

A generation or two, and the Tennessee valley was in the 1920s, the 1930s.

During this period, throughout the great river basin, in cities like Knoxville, on the farms and plantations of the cotton belt, and on the steep slopes of the southern mountains, there hung a great pall of despair. The national depression of the 1930s was responsible only in part. Somehow, somewhere in the past, this great Southern valley had been left behind in the nation's forward march, for poor land has always been reflected in poor living. Now, after only a few generations, both the people and the earth were destitute.

Let us take another look to determine what had become of the farms and mines, of the sharecroppers and tenants, of the out-of-touch hill folk.

Recall Ducktown. Famed Ducktown had become infamous. Standing high on a hill was the huge smelter, roasting the ore and belching clouds of sulfur fumes into the air. These poisonous gases spread out over the surrounding countryside. A tourist guide written in the 1930s described the view: "Ramshackle houses are huddled below the smelter's giant walls. Deep gullies

extend into the village from the surrounding badlands."
Another visitor saw this: "From the road the scene is one
of utter desolation. Even the soil has taken the copper
color and there is not a tree or even a blade of grass."

The outlook in the bituminous coal fields, scattered
over 40,000 square miles of the southern Appalachians,
had also become drearier and drearier. In the 1930s
Bruce Crawford described the conditions of the miners
there in a book called *Culture of the South*:

> At the average mine, the lot of the miner and his fam-
> ily has been unspeakable poverty: a hovel for shelter,
> poorest clothing, an incredible diet, no sanitation, indif-
> ferent medical attention; emaciation, untimely death . . .

> The miner's home in the average camp is anything but
> "home, sweet home." The houses are, for the most part,
> crudely constructed shacks, closely set in rows along
> hillsides or creek bottoms. The worst are without plaster,
> running water, toilets, or sanitation of any kind. Cracks
> in the walls are covered with newspapers plastered on
> with flour paste to keep out the winter winds. Water is
> carried from springs in roadsides or creek banks. The
> privy is built over a creek, or on the slope near the back
> door. The cow, when the miner is so fortunate as to own
> one, is stabled under the floor if the house is one of those
> perched on stilts upon the hillside. Sanitation is prac-
> tically non-existent.

The miners and their families had scarcely enough to
eat.

> Cornbread made with water, while it may sometimes
> be esteemed as part of a repast, is certainly neither whole-

some nor toothsome when taken as a steady diet. Potatoes may be found prepared two ways, fried and mashed, for the same meal, with little else. Pumpkins, which farmer's raise for their livestock but which they share with the miner, are served two or three different ways for a single meal. Not always is there milk, even canned milk, for the children. Any cows the miners may own go dry from lack of fodder.

Conditions in the coal industry were but one example. In the years following the Civil War the eyes of Northern industrialists had turned increasingly toward the South. The South continued to offer untold and unexploited natural resources, potential water power, a favorable climate. Above all, it offered a large, cheap labor force. An increasingly industrialized "New South" had emerged.

The cotton industry, for instance, had steadily shifted from New England to the cotton-growing states of the South. In 1850 New England had 74 percent of the cotton-spinning spindles; the South 6.6 percent. By 1915 New England had 53 percent, while the South had 40. And the curve kept shifting steadily.

Now small farmers in the valley—who had found it impossible to raise enough corn on the steep, eroding hills—were turning to the textile mills looking for work. So, too, were those who had formerly picked tobacco or cotton in the lowlands, for the chance of making a living from the leaves and bolls of these crops grew more and more difficult, what with periodic floods, blights, and poor soil.

Corn was grown on the hilly acres
of this farm near
Oliver Springs, Tennessee.

What was the lot of mill workers in the new, industrializing South? We have this description about conditions in the early years of the new century from Dr. Howard Odum's *The Way of the South:*

Early morning, and thousands of mill folk rising and going to work at the call of the mill whistle. . . .

Pictures of moving activity; here they come to work. If it is summer, the morning is light and one sees men and women, girls and boys, coming hurriedly from every direction. In the adjacent countryside the mill workers' kinsfolk on the farm start for the fields. If it is winter, the workers are heeding the call of the mill whistle though the visitor cannot see them because of the darkness of the early morning. Five hundred, one thousand, two thousand, five thousand strong they come. These people of ages from fourteen to fifty, of farm and mountain heritage for the most part, come teeming in to their new-found work. The men come clad in overalls, or a three-dollar pair of trousers and a coat which does not match. The women and girls clad in dresses of gingham or of similar material, the older ones sometimes with the cotton lint from the previous day's work still clinging to their hair, hurry to the spinning or spooling department, or to the weave shop. And back home again, and tomorrow like today, unless to move to another mill.

The new textile industry drew hundreds of thousands from farm and mountain valley to the mill village. One reason for locating such manufacturing in the South was that the raw material—cotton—was nearby. And most of it was still being cultivated and picked by hand

—in the style of slavery days—by the tenants and croppers.

A social worker, Lillian Perrine Davis, was sent by
Survey Graphic magazine to study the Southern sharecroppers and farm laborers a few years after the stock
market collapse of 1929. Her conclusion was that these
people—"the lowest dregs of our southern agricultural
system"—were not depression victims. Rather, they had
continued "depressed" from generation to generation.

*They live in tumbledown shanties, many of them with-
out even windows, on erosion-swept farms, where they
have been used to receive for the labor of the entire
family—grandmothers, fathers, sons, five-year-old children, pregnant mothers—an annual income which runs
from the high peak of thirty-five dollars down to nothing
at all. And when I say nothing I mean just that. Often
and often they gather their two or three skimpy bales of
cotton; pay one half of it for rent; pay their government
loans or their store accounts, as the case may be; and have
left not one penny to carry them through till spring when
they can begin drawing supplies against a new crop—if
they are lucky enough to have a crop . . .*

They bathe in a little tin washpan, without privacy,
towels or soap. They eat with their fingers because they
have no forks. They never saw a mattress until the government gave them one, sleeping three and four in a
bed on straw-filled ticks, or else rolled in a ragged quilt
on the floor. They wear dirty clothes because they have
none into which they can change. Their babies die of
"summer complaint" because they have no screens, no

". . . also the bag, which can hold a hundred pounds,
is filled as it is dragged from plant to plant . . ."
—James Agee.

knowledge of sanitation, no heart to fend away a fate which from long standing appears to them inevitable. They drink branch water charged with typhoid because there is none able, or willing, to buy them a well bucket. Their teeth ache and rot and fall away because there are no free clinics and no way to stretch a zero income to include dental fees. They are sick with despair and call it the ague, tuberculosis, or simply "weakness" and "spells." And never from birth to death do they ever know what it means to wear comfortable clothing or have a sufficiency of food.

From birth to death, from one generation to the next, the grinding, sweating, sun-up to sun-down work of cotton growing and harvesting went on and on.

In the 1930s writer James Agee lived among the tenants and croppers, and wrote a book about them called *Let Us Now Praise Famous Men*. He gave a word-picture of cotton picking, the culminating activity of a year's grueling labor.

It is simple and terrible work. Skill will help you; all the endurance you can draw up against it from the roots of your existence will be thoroughly used as fuel to it; but neither skill nor endurance can make it any easier.

Over the right shoulder you have slung a long white sack whose half length trails the ground behind. You work with both hands as fast and steadily as you can . . .

Meanwhile, too, you are working in a land of sunlight and heat which are special to just such country at just that time of year: sunlight that stands and stacks itself upon you with the serene weight of deep water, and heat that makes the jointed and muscled and fine-structured body glow like one indiscriminate oil; and this brilliant weight of heat is piled upon you more and more heavily in hour after hour . . . also the bag, which can hold a hundred pounds, is filling as it is dragged from plant to plant . . . and the sack still heavier and heavier, so that it pulls you back as a beast might rather than a mere dead weight; but it is not only this: cotton plants are low, so that in this heat and burden of the imminent sun and of the heavying sack you are dragging, you are continuously somewhat stooped over even if you are a child, and are bent very deep if you are a man or a woman. A strong back is a godsend, but not even the strongest back was built for that treatment . . .

Agee drew sensitive individual portraits of the share-croppers and tenant farmers he met. Their very persons reflected their labor and their poverty. One was George Gudger; the writer described him, a little uncomfortable in his Sunday best, like this:

Sunday, George Gudger:
   Freshly laundered cotton gauze underwear.
   Mercerized blue green socks, held up over his fist-like calves by scraps of pink and green gingham rag.
   Long bulb-toed black shoes; still shining with the glaze of their first newness, streaked with clay.
   Trousers of a hard and cheap cotton-wool, dark blue with narrow gray stripes; a twenty-five-cent belt stays in them always.
   A freshly laundered and brilliantly starched white shirt with narrow black stripes.

A brown, green, and gold tie in broad stripes, of stiff and hard imitation watered silk. . . .

The crease is still sharp in the trousers.

If he were an older man, and faithful in the rural tradition of dressing well rather than in that of the young men in towns, he would wear, not a belt, but suspenders, striped, or perhaps decorated with rosebuds.

These are the only socks he owns. . . .

He walks a little carefully: the shoes hurt his feet.

The wives of croppers and tenants worked alongside their husbands in the fields. They also managed the house and pieced together by hand clothes for the family. Among those Agee wrote of was:

Mrs. Ricketts: I am not sure that she has more than one work dress; in any case there was no change of it during the time that I knew her, and it seemed even at the first to have been worn for a long time. Excepting for the clothes of babies, it is the most primitive sewn and designed garment I have ever seen. It is made of a coarse tan cotton I will speak of later. It is shaped like a straight-sided bell, with a little hole at the top for the head to stick through, the cloth slit from the neck to below the breasts and held together if I remember rightly with a small snarl of shoelace; the bare arms sticking through the holes at the sides, the skirt ending a little below the knee, the whole dress standing out a little from the body on all sides like a child's youngest cartoons, not belted, and too stiffened perhaps with dirt to fall into any folds other than the broadest and plainest, the skirt so broad away from her at the bottom that, with her little feet and legs standing down from inside it, for all their beauty they seem comic sticks, and she, a grievous resemblance to newspaper drawings of timid men in barrels labeled John Q. Public.

The plight of the Gudgers, Ricketts, and others even less fortunate was expressed in the folk music they sang:

Raggedy

Rag - gedy, rag - gedy are we, Just as rag - gedy, rag - gedy can be, Well we don't get noth-ing for our la-bor, So rag - gedy, rag - gedy are we.

Hungry, hungry are we,
Just as hungry, hungry can be,
Well we don't get nothing for our labor,
So hungry, hungry are we.

Homeless, homeless are we,
Just as homeless, homeless can be,
Well we don't get nothing for our labor,
So homeless, homeless are we.

Landless, landless are we,
Just as landless, landless can be,
So landless, landless are we.
Well we don't get nothing for our labor,

Pitiful, so pitiful are we,
Just as pitiful, pitiful can be,
Well we don't get nothing for our labor,
So pitiful, pitiful are we.

REPEAT FIRST STANZA

These were white tenants and croppers, but what of the black croppers? Their lot was similar—or harder, for they suffered from racism carried over from the days of slavery. Violent episodes marked the 1930s, but the everyday uneasiness between white and black neighbors is as well conveyed in a simple scene Agee described. He had seen a Negro couple walking along the road:

They were fifty yards or so up the road, walking leisurely . . . He was in dark trousers, black dress shoes, a new laundered white shirt with lights of bluing in it, and a light yellow, soft straw hat with a broad band of dark flowered cloth and a daisy in the band; she glossy-legged without stockings, in freshly whited pumps, a flowered pink cotton dress, and a great sun of straw set far back on her head.

Wanting to speak to them, Agee ran after them. Their response reflected generations of fear.

At the sound of the twist of my shoe to the gravel, the young woman's whole body was jerked down tight as a fist into a crouch . . . [and then] she sprang forward into the first motions of a running not human but that of a suddenly terrified wild animal. In this same instant the young man froze . . . [then] hurried to her and put his hand on her flowered shoulder and, inclining his head forward and sidewise as if listening, spoke with her, and they lifted, and watched me while, shaking my head, and raising my palm outward, I came up to them . . . "I'm very sorry! I'm very sorry if I scared you! . . ."

Not only racial fears, but misfortunes of the land fell with special impact on the Negro tenants and croppers. Listen to their song about the boll weevil—despoiler of the cotton crop:

The Ballad of the Boll Weevil

The first time I seen the boll wee-vil, I seen him in New York, Next time I seen the boll wee-vil, He was climb-ing up a cot-ton stalk, Just look-in' for a home,

Just look-in' for a home, Just look-in' for a home, Just look-in' for a home.____

The first time I seen the boll weevil,
He was settin' on the square,
The next time I seen the boll weevil,
He had all his family there,
    Just lookin' for a home, etc.

The farmer took the boll weevil,
And buried him in the sand,
Boll weevil said to the farmer,
"I'll stand it like a man,
    It'll be my home," etc.

Then the farmer took the boll weevil,
And left him on the ice,
Boll weevil say to the farmer,
"This is mighty cool and nice,
    It'll be my home," etc.

Farmer said to the boll weevil,
"I see you at my door,"
"Yessir," said the boll weevil,
"I been here before,
    I'm gonna get your home," etc.

Boll weevil say to the farmer,
"You can ride in your Ford machine,
When I get through with yo' cotton,
Can't buy no gasoline,
    Won't have no home," etc.

The farmer say to the merchant,
"I want some meat and meal,"
"Get away from here you son of a gun,
Got weevils in yo' field,
    Gonna get yo' home," etc.

If anyone should ask you
Who it was that wrote this song,
Tell him 'twas a dark-skinned farmer
With a pair of blue duckin's on,
    Lookin' for a home
    Just lookin' for a home, etc.

Miners, mill workers, tenants, and croppers, these were the most oppressed and downtrodden people of the valley. There were others, the "middle folk"—preachers and teachers, doctors and lawyers, small farmers and owners of small businesses. But life even for middle folk was hard in the rural South. Dr. Howard Odum described a stripling who somehow managed to get a medical education:

For forty years he carried on a practice so immense and so widely scattered that it would drive three modern medicos into nervous prostration in six months. The horses the man drove to death would have remounted a regiment of cavalry; and in the vast, poverty-smitten region over which he ranged, not one patient in five could ever pay him a cent. He could hardly buy a decent coat, not to mention expensive surgical equipment; yet I doubt that he slept a single night through for half a lifetime. Through sleet and snow on many a bitter night alcohol carried him through when he must otherwise have failed some suffering pauper in the remote wilderness.

Another exception was Jesse Stuart, a teacher in a one-room school. Today a distinguished writer, Jesse Stuart began teaching in the mid-1920s in the hill country of eastern Kentucky—an area outside the valley strictly considered, but with a similar way of life. In a book called *The Thread That Runs So True*, he wrote about his own experiences, and especially about the children of small farmers and middle folk. It was a life that still carried strains of the early settlers', while the rest of America's children listened to Blondie and Dagwood on the radio and saw Babe Ruth in movie newsreels.

About his first class, he wrote,

I had from the beginners to the eighth grade, all in one room. This was so in every rural school in Greenwood County. I had never thought about this until I had started teaching . . .

I thought we had reached the schoolhouse very early. It wasn't eight o'clock and school didn't start until eight-thirty. The July sun hadn't dried the dew from parts of the valley yet; dew was ascending in white formless clouds from the tobacco, cane, and corn patches. But the people in Lonesome Valley went to bed early and got up early. All of the pupils in Lonesome Valley came from farms.

The girls wore pigtails down their backs tied with all colors of ribbons. They wore clean print dresses and they were barefooted. Not one pupil in my school, large or small, boy or girl, wore a pair of shoes. I'd never seen in my life so many barefooted people, young, middle-aged, and old, as I had seen in Lonesome Valley. Wearing gloves on their hands in summer was the same to them as wearing shoes on their feet. They just didn't do it.

The school had neither electricity nor water, even from a well. Water had to be carried in a bucket from a neighbor's home, and all the children drank from a common dipper. So Jesse Stuart made "an important announcement" to his pupils. He told them that

each had to bring his own drinking cup the next day. It could be a glass, teacup, gourd, dipper, just so it was his own and no one else drank from it. My pupils looked at one another and laughed as if my announcement was funny. But I had seen sweat run from their faces into the dipper, and the next in line put his mouth where the sweat had run or where the other pupil had put his lips. I noticed, too, several pupils had put the rim up near the handle to their mouths, so I knew they didn't like to drink after the others.

On Tuesday they brought their dippers, tin cups, and glasses. Only a few had forgotten, and I stopped with my busy schedule of class work long enough to teach them how to make paper drinking cups. I showed them how to take a clean sheet of paper from a tablet and fold it to hold water. I gave them a lecture about drinking water. I told them never to drink from a stream. I told them how I had gotten typhoid fever twice: once from drinking cool water from a little stream, and once from drinking in a river. I had my pupils use the dipper to dip water from the bucket into their cups. They

*Lewis Hine photographed school
in session at Loyston, Tennessee, in the fall of 1933.
Note the pot-bellied stove.*

accepted my suggestion gladly. I also borrowed another water bucket from Bertha Conway and brought it to school. The one bucket allowed me for thirty-five pupils (and there would be more as soon as the farmers were through with their summer plowing and worming and suckering tobacco, stripping their cane and boiling the juice to syrup) was not enough. They played hard at recess and noon and in the "time of books" sat in a schoolroom almost as hot as a stove oven.

The summer passed and fall came. Stuart writes:

The sea of multicolored leaves [was] whipped from the Lonesome Valley trees by the raw and biting November winds. The two great furrows, turned in opposite directions by some great mythical plow in the beginning of time to make narrow-gauged Lonesome Valley, were naked, grotesque, and ugly now.

But despite the icy winds, he continues,

My attendance grew. And to show you that my pupils loved to come to school, many came thinly clad and barefooted, after the white frosts had fallen and had blanketed the frozen land. For the farmers hadn't sold their tobacco crops yet. They usually sold them about Christmas time, and this was their "money crop." Many times I saw the red spots on the white frost from the bleeding little bare feet of those who came to school regardless of shoes . . .

We crowded close to the potbellied stove. We fired it until it was red-hot. The heat from it hurt our eyes. And now we wished for the evenness of the July heat.

We knew we could bear the July heat more easily than we could the screaming fury of icy wind that continued to smite Lonesome Valley. The corners of our schoolroom were cold . . .

In Lonesome Valley of the 1920s Jesse Stuart participated in corn husking and square dancing and sorghum making not far removed from the frolicking of a century earlier. He describes one evening when

We listened to this local band play with their banjos, fiddles, guitar, mandolin, and accordion from seven until eleven. They never played the same tune twice, and often when they played a fast breakdown, one of the listeners would dance. I had never heard old-time music sound as beautiful as this . . .

There was hardly a family in this big vicinity who didn't have a musician. This was part of their recreation. People had learned to play musical instruments to furnish their own music just as they had learned to plant, cultivate, and harvest crops for their food supply. They depended upon themselves for practically everything.

I went with my pupils, their parents, and neighbors to cornhuskings, apple-peelings, bean-stringings, square dances, and to the belling of the bride when there was a wedding. Often we rode mules many miles through darkness or moonlight to these community events. I never missed a party at the mill when they made sorghum molasses in this great cane country. We went to the sorghum mill, shoved each other in the skimmings-hole and ate the soft sweet foam from the boiling cane juice with long paddles whittled from willow wood.

Sorghum molasses and cane foam were for the children, and for the older folks corn liquor was still being brewed in the hills. With one eye out for revenuers, jugs were filled and voices raised:

Copper Kettle

Get you a cop - per ket - tle. ____

Get you a cop - per coil. ____

Fill it with new made corn - mash, ____ And

nev - er more you'll toil. *Chorus* You'll just lay there

by the ju - ni - per, ____ While the

moon ____ is bright. ____ Watch the jugs a

fill - in' ____ in the pale ____ moon-light.

Build your fire with hickory,
Hickory, ash, and oak.
Don't use no green or rotten wood,
They'll catch you by the smoke.

CHORUS

My daddy, he made whiskey,
And my granddaddy did, too.
We ain't paid a whiskey tax
Since seventeen-ninety-two.

CHORUS

The people of Lonesome Valley and of most of the
Tennessee River basin were living in a world apart from
the rest of the nation. They had been for nearly a century. Then with the coming of the great depression in
1929 the whole country was plunged into despair, and as
for the valley, the pall of privation finally enveloped it
completely. The depression took its relentless toll in the
mountainous regions and in the bottomlands too. Thousands of miners of the rich coal beds of Appalachia were
idle and desperate as the boom of World War I gave
way to the bust of the early 1930s. Thousands of farm
families came close to starvation on their worn-out,
steep-sloping acres. The average yearly income of the
farm families growing cotton on flatter land fell to $216.

Voicing the farmers' personal distress during the depression days were letters such as this one, written by the
wife of a sharecropper to the Southern Tenant Farmers'
Union:

Making sorghum molasses,
as photographed by Hine.

Mr. Mitchell, Sir i am written to you to let you no how we are gettinge along. our landlord compelling husbon to morgage his crop and stock to get finish 1936 . . . i am tirde all ready and gather 9 Bals of Cotton 1935 and get nothen but $30 tax. that is what we had to pay after indebt was paid. You no i am tirde wearing cotton sack, flour sack. i am in kneed, children in kneed, house in kneed . . . i am lookinge to hear from soon. very sincerely,

Glennie French

Numbers in the Tennessee valley were rendered homeless by the disaster of the great depression. A writer working for the Federal Writers Project during the 1930s took down the story of one woman who was reduced to living as a squatter on the Tennessee River bottom when it was low season at Knoxville.

Fan Flanigan sat against one of the crooked sapling poles which supported the driftwood joists of the porch. She was a small wizened woman, brown, gnarled, with thin gray hair.

"It's all right here," she said, "and I like it pretty fair as long as the river don't start acting up. We don't have no rent to pay, jest sort of squat here betwixt the railroad tracks and the water and build our places out of what we can get off the dump and the wood we can ketch floating down the river. Me and Mammy have been here sence nineteen and thirty-two, that hard old year."

She puckered her eyes against the strong sunlight and glanced over the thirteen stilt-set shanties which strag-

Eroded land, eroded lives—
this photograph was taken in East Tennessee in 1939.

gled along the banks of the Tennessee River between the approaches to two of Knoxville's bridges . . .

"You kind of grow to like this place," said Fan Flanigan. "A rich man up to Knoxville give this whole strip betwixt the bridges for poor folks to build they houses on."

Fan Flanigan went on to explain that she and her mother received eleven dollars a month from the latter's old-age pension.

"It's what we live on. Besides that, we get supplies off the relief, stuff out of the garden when a drouth or a rise don't hit it.

"But Great Day! When the river rises they's no chance for a garden then. High water will drown a garden right to death. And we do get high water here off and on and the water kivers the whole place."

"The water," Fan Flanigan had said. Clearly the poverty of the valley was in part due to entrenched old ways —row-crop farming, poor schooling, and industrial exploitation. All these things the great depression had thrown into sharp relief. But it was also due to the fact that the Tennessee River itself, with all its resource possibilities, had not yet been tamed or utilized at all to bring a better life to the valley's people.

Instead, the Tennessee had remained as turbulent and fitful as it had been when the pioneer Donelson party went down it by flatboat. But now it was twentieth-century America, and one might rightfully have expected a river to bring abundance to its valley and its people. A navigable waterway would have provided for commercial transportation, and a properly dammed river would have made the generation of electricity possible through hydro-power. Wisely used as a resource, the Tennessee River need not have inundated the valley's acres and washed away its soil, but might instead have served to make the river basin green and fruitful, and its people prosperous.

All the potential was there, but was anything being done about it? Were there any who were concerned with reclaiming and restoring the valley's natural resources?

☆ | 3 | ☆

THE USE OF THE EARTH FOR
THE GOOD OF MAN

There turned out to be one possible way of stopping this tragic waste of human and natural resources, and it sprang from the organized efforts of a group of people known as conservationists.

Conservation as a movement began in the early 1900s. Even then, there was little direct knowledge of the relationship between one natural resource and another, though a few thoughtful and observant men were beginning to note it. One day, in the winter of 1907, Gifford Pinchot, chief forester under President Theodore Roosevelt, was taking a solitary ride through a park in the nation's capital. Perhaps he recalled these words of Thomas Jefferson: "The indifferent state of agriculture among us does not proceed from want of knowledge merely; it is from our having such quantities of land to waste as we please." But the westward-moving settlers and empire builders had shrugged and answered, "Why worry, there will always be more."

Pinchot wondered what was the relationship—for there must be one—between forestry and other resources: streams, soil, minerals, fish, and game. Did not forestry have some direct connection with floods and soil erosion? These questions would not let him be.

He wrote in *Breaking New Ground:*

Here were not isolated and separate problems. My work had brought me into touch with all of them. But what was the basic link between them?

Suddenly the idea flashed through my head that there was a unity in this complication—that the relation of one resource to another was not the end of the story. Here were no longer a lot of different, independent, and often antagonistic questions, each on its own separate little island, as we had been in the habit of thinking. In place of them, here was one single question with many parts. Seen in this new light, all these separate questions fitted into and made up the one great central problem of the use of the earth for the good of man.

This flash of insight ushered in a new concept of resource use—conservation.

The movement itself was officially born at a White House conference called by President Theodore Roosevelt on May 13, 1908. A commission was appointed to make an inventory of the nation's resources, its waters, soil, forests, and minerals. The "brains" of the commission were two of the leaders of the early conservation movement, forester Gifford Pinchot and WJ "No Stop" McGee, anthropologist, geologist, and hydrologist.

The inventory was made, and President Roosevelt said of it: "As it stands, it is an irrefutable proof that the conservation of our resources is the fundamental question

Gifford Pinchot.

before this Nation, and that our first and greatest task is to set our house in order and begin to live within our means."

Another early step in the conservation movement was the formation of the Inland Waterways Commission. Its policy was revolutionary: a river was no longer to be regarded as either a segmented waterway or a private property but rather as "a unit from source to sea." The commission recommended that "hereafter any plans for the use of inland waterways in connection with interstate commerce shall regard the streams of the country as an asset of the people, shall take full account of the conservation of all resources connected with running waters and shall look to the protection of these resources from monopoly and to their administration in the interests of the people."

Such ideas were by no means popular. There were many who believed that the individual owner of property adjacent to a river had full rights, under state sovereignty, to use and develop water power without federal interference. To them, the concepts of Teddy Roosevelt and his conservationist "fanatics" were not only "legally absurd but socially immoral." Captain William Patrick Lay, of the Alabama Power Company, spoke up for private enterprise as he understood it:

The fundamental principles underlying our form of government, holding sacred private property, private rights and privileges, have weathered the storm of ages. Why are we now called on to abandon those safe-and-sound moorings, follow off after false Gods and branch out into untried fields of theory?

*We must insist that, on the sanctity of private prop-
erty, our constitution and laws, more than all else, de-
pends our proper future progress.*

This was the view not only of utility executives but of
most of official Washington and a majority of Congress
as well. They admitted only one exception—the control
of navigation in the interest of national security.

It was not long afterward that the advent of World
War I presented just such an emergency. Nitrates were
needed for munitions, and the government required
"nitrogen-fixing" plants. Though free nitrogen is abundant—four-fifths of the atmosphere—it cannot be used
for explosives. It must first be "fixed."

The world has only one large source of natural fixed
nitrogen—South America's sodium nitrate or Chile salt-
peter beds. Already, as World War I approached, Ger-
many, in particular, was afraid that impending war would
cut off access to the Chilean nitrate beds. A German
professor, Dr. Fritz Haber, found a way of forcing
nitrogen and hydrogen gases into combination to form
ammonia, and his method was called the Haber process.

Meanwhile, scientists in the United States were developing the cyanamid process: heated air, with its large
percentage of free nitrogen, was shot over hot calcium
carbide in an electric furnace. The resulting calcium and
carbon compound could subsequently be converted to
nitrates.

Both these processes were still in an experimental
stage when the United States entered World War I, yet

nitrogen-fixing plants had to be set up without delay. Who would operate them, the government or private enterprise?

In 1916 the Sixty-fourth Congress passed the National Defense Act, giving the President power to investigate and determine "the best, cheapest, and most available means in the production of nitrates . . . for munitions of war and useful in the manufacture of fertilizers." (Ironically, the compounds of nitrogen called nitrates provide both the sinews of war—explosives—and the nutrients of peace—fertilizers.) The President was empowered to select sites, and the plants were to be constructed and operated solely by the government, not by private enterprise.

The use of hydroelectric power was considered essential to keep down the costs of manufacturing nitrogen compounds. But where was the power to come from? One possibility was the as yet untamed water of the Tennessee River as it passed through Muscle Shoals. A gradual but steady drop of 134 feet—only 21 feet shy of the sheer drop at Niagara Falls—such was the power potential of the stretch of river at Muscle Shoals.

With the United States declaration of war in April 1917, Muscle Shoals was quickly chosen as the site. Two nitrogen-fixing plants were constructed under government contract and ownership. One plant was set up to make ammonia using what little was known of the Haber process; the other was designed for the cyanamid process. Great Wilson Dam was begun to supply hydropower for the plants.

But the Haber plant was a failure from the start, and

the cyanamid plant was scarcely ready for operation when the war ended. Wilson Dam was half-finished, and because of delay in appropriating funds, the dam, 137 feet high and almost a mile long, was not completed until 1925.

But now the war was over. The familiar question arose again. Who would operate the Muscle Shoals properties: the government or private enterprise? Under the National Defense Act, the properties were to be government-operated even in peacetime to make fertilizers, and *cheap* fertilizers were badly needed. On the other hand, advances in science had already made the cyanamid process obsolete, and an improved Haber process had been snapped up by private industry. In a way, the Muscle Shoals plants and the dam were now "white elephants."

There was great pressure to dispose of the plants and power potential to private interests, either by lease or by sale. Chemical companies, power companies, and others bid; the offer most seriously considered was made by industrialist Henry Ford. No fewer than 138 bills were introduced in Congress on the subject.

These bills came before the Senate Committee on Agriculture, headed by Senator George Norris of Nebraska, a Republican who called himself a "fighting liberal." Senator Norris and his committee realized that a precedent far more significant than the disposition of two plants and a dam was involved in Muscle Shoals. They foresaw the advantages that would accrue to the nation if the Tennessee and other large rivers were harnessed and developed "for the people." Norris wrote,

*I was impressed by the periodical floods exacting such
an enormous toll in sections of the United States . . .*

*I had come to the conclusion that many of the
streams in the United States, flowing from the mountains, through the meadows to the sea, presented the
opportunity to produce great amounts of electricity for
the homes and factories of the nation.*

River development would mean better navigation and
irrigation in regions where water was scarce. All these
things—flood control, generation and development of
electricity, navigation, irrigation—were in Norris' view
"inseparably linked."

It would be a battle, however. Norris wrote, "The
early twenties brought the American people to their
knees in worship at the shrine of private business and
industry. It was said, and accepted without question by
millions of Americans, that private enterprise could do
no wrong."

But if the Ford offer were to be accepted, Norris said,

*then the fight for conservation that has been waged by
public-spirited and patriotic men and women all over the
country is not only lost and given away but those who
are unwillingly compelled to make the gift are to be
taxed 100 years to make the gift more profitable. It is
the greatest gift ever bestowed upon mortal man since
salvation was made free to the human race.*

Ford himself stepped out of the picture in 1924, but
actually even his withdrawal did not end it. Rather, two
great national calamities did.

The first was the violent rampaging of the nation's largest river. Nothing new, but suddenly the whole country was awakened to the frightful damage done. In the spring of 1927, *The New York Times* carried this story:

New Orleans, May 8. *The battle to hold the last sector in the Mississippi levee line from Cairo to New Orleans is under way. So far the great river racing south with a crest the highest in history, leaving in its wake and the wake of its flooded tributaries the greatest area of devastation and destruction the nation has ever known, has won every phase of the conflict.*

Herbert Hoover, then Secretary of Commerce, was on the scene in Louisiana.

Tonight [he said], there are 192,000 destitute men, women and children in the [improvised] camps of the American Red Cross, and there are 134,000 others whose plight is just as pathetic on the roofs of houses and the upper floors of such buildings as have not been swept away by the flood waters. All of these 326,000 unfortunate American citizens are being fed and otherwise cared for by the Red Cross.
But vast as is this army of unfortunates the end is not yet, for more hundreds are coming to us for aid with the passing of each day . . .

A song of the era told what it was like to be flooded out:

Backwater Blues

It rained five days and the sky turned dark as night_
It rained five days and the
sky turned dark as night — There was
trou - ble tak - ing place in the low __ land that night.

I woke up this morning, wouldn't even get out of my door
I woke up this morning, wouldn't even get out of my door
Enough trouble to make a poor girl wonder where she gonna go.

It thundered and it lightened and the winds began to blow
It thundered and it lightened and the winds began to blow
There was a thousand women didn't have no place to go.

I went out to the lonesome, high old lonesome hill
I went out to the lonesome, high old lonesome hill
I looked down on the old house where I used to live.

Backwater Blues have caused me to pack up my things and go
Backwater Blues have caused me to pack up my things and go
Cause my house fell down and I can't live there no more.

Mmm I can't live there no more
Mmm I can't live there no more
And there ain't a place for a poor old girl to go.

They rowed a little boat about five miles 'cross me farm
They rowed a little boat about five miles 'cross me farm
I packed up all my clothing—throwed it in and they rowed
  me along.

Words and music by Huddie Ledbetter, TRO © 1963, Folkways Music Publishers, Inc., New York, New York. Used by permission.

Huge areas in the valley of the Mississippi River were devastated. And because the watershed of the "Father of Waters" extended north and south from the Great Lakes to the Gulf of Mexico, east and west from the Appalachians to the Rockies, the destructive and periodic flooding of its waters was of far more than local concern. Investigations that followed by the Corps of Engineers and Congress enlightened national thinking. It was no longer adequate to think only in terms of levees strung mile after mile along the Mississippi. Instead, the waters in the upper reaches of the rivers feeding the Mississippi, the tributaries, would have to be regulated and controlled too. The Tennessee River was one such tributary.

The flood of 1927 was a national tragedy. It was the first calamity, but it was not enough. Just one year after the great flood, Senator Norris introduced his fifth bill regarding control of the Tennessee River. It was pocket-vetoed by President Coolidge.

Meanwhile, Wilson Dam at Muscle Shoals, "the greatest mass of masonry so far compiled by man," remained idle. *The New York Times* reported on April 20, 1930:

*Wreckage from a
Tennessee River flood of 1927.*

The idling is what most impresses you. You see a magnificent parade of masonry across nearly a mile of river. Transforming station, power house, dam and locks step out together in an architectural line as splendid and formidable as if mountains marched. On one side is a lake, Lake Wilson, eighteen miles long. On the other are swirling cascades with a sheer drop of ninety feet, the difference between the two levels. Somewhere in the narrow space between, turbines with the strength of 30,000 horses churn the force and fall of the water into transmissible power more nonchalantly than a pan of milk is whipped into butter.

It was only water going over the dam, not power or electricity. The people of the Tennessee valley saw the wastage and were dejected. On June 18, 1930, Senator Hugo Black of Alabama received a telegram:

FLORENCE, ALA. TELEGRAM YOU RECEIVED FROM MUSCLE SHOALS THIS MORNING FRAMED BY CITY FATHERS, IN CITY HALL, BY LIGHT OF KEROSENE LAMPS, THOUGH WITHIN TWO MILES OF TREMENDOUS POWER TUMBLING TO WASTE OVER WILSON DAM WITH ADMINISTRATION'S CONSENT. JUDGE FRED JOHNSON, JR.

Senator Black inserted the telegram into the *Congressional Record*.

But again, in March 1931, another Tennessee River bill, passed by both houses of Congress, was vetoed by the White House. President Hoover said of the project, "That is not liberalism, it is degeneration."

Then, in the 1930s, came the second influential calam-

ANOTHER GEORGE W. TRYING TO CROSS THE DELAWARE.

ity: the great depression following the stock market crash of 1929. This disaster swept into office Franklin D. Roosevelt, who as President pledged a "new deal" for the American people. This, he felt, entailed a government more active in the life of the nation.

Roosevelt had himself been a practicing conservationist for years. Among his personal letters was this one, written a few days after he took office.

To Nelson C. Brown, New York State College of Forestry, Syracuse University, Syracuse, New York
[Washington] March 8, 1933

My Dear Nelson: As you know, the State College of Forestry has carried on tree plantings on the experimental acreage on my Creek Road Farm at Hyde Park for each of the last two years. As we are getting close to the tree-planting season again I wish you would take up with your associates the planting of an additional acreage next month.

I have instructed William Plog, my mother's superintendent at Hyde Park, to have about five acres now in birch growth, cleared, and there is also other available land on the other side of the road. I am wholly willing to leave it to the College as to what type of trees to put in this year, as you will be able to continue the scheme of things started in 1931 . . .

I wish you would make a note of having a careful inspection made of the swamp area planted last year. The permanent tree crop consisted of tulip poplars and black walnuts and these were interspaced with, I think, red

A *Washington* Evening Star *cartoon.*

67

cedar and larch. This planting must be filled out to replace trees that have died. During the winter I had all the sprouts cut off from the stumps of the old trees that had been cut.

Always sincerely yours,

[Franklin D. Roosevelt]

Conservation oriented—a "tree grower" he once called himself—Roosevelt, as one of his first measures, established the Civilian Conservation Corps to replant the nation's forests. In the CCC Roosevelt saw a way of restoring people as well as restoring the land, both together. Some 300,000 young men would be given employment. At the same time, what was badly needed work for them would tie in with the "conservation of our forests, providing for increased and better tree crops, eliminating destructive floods and preventing soil erosion."

President Roosevelt also had a lively interest in regional resource planning, and he had had his eye on the Tennessee valley in particular for some time.

Before I came to Washington [he wrote] I had decided that for many reasons the Tennessee Valley—in other words, all of the watershed of the Tennessee River and its tributaries—would provide an ideal location for a land use experiment on a regional scale embracing many states.

In January I visited Muscle Shoals with a group of officials and experts . . .

Senator Norris had been of course one of the officials at Roosevelt's side. He heard the President-elect make a public promise that the development of the Tennessee valley through the harnessing of its river would indeed go forward full steam in his administration. As they stood together watching the waters of the Tennessee swirl through the floodgates of Wilson Dam, Roosevelt said, "This should be a happy day for you, George." "It is, Mr. President," replied the senator, "I see my dreams come true."

What had originally been Norris' vision turned out to be one of the most successful and ambitious of Roosevelt's New Deal programs: the Tennessee Valley Act. The act was passed in the spring of 1933. It created the Tennessee Valley Authority and provided for the first and only unified source-to-mouth treatment of a great river and its tributaries that our nation has ever undertaken. The act provided for flood control by a series of dams and reservoirs; development of navigation; generation of electricity by using the potential of falling water; use of marginal lands; reforestation of all lands in the basin suitable for reforestation; and economic and social well-being of the people living in the river basin.

Be it enacted by the Senate and House of Representatives of the United States of America in Congress assembled, that for the purposes of maintaining and operating the properties now owned by the United States in the vicinity of Muscle Shoals, Alabama, in the interest of the national defense and for agricultural and industrial development, and to improve navigation on the Tennessee River and to control the destructive flood waters in the Tennessee River and Mississippi River Basins, *there is hereby created a body corporate by the name of the Tennessee Valley Authority.*

With these official words a dream became a reality. A bitter debate yielded to the long, hard task of harnessing a mighty river and changing the fortunes of the people who lived within its reaches. The fight was over; the victory won. Every dam and steamplant in the giant, river-harnessing system created by TVA would carry this prominent inscription: "BUILT FOR THE PEOPLE OF THE UNITED STATES."

☆ | 4 | ☆

"THEM GUVMENT FELLERS"

Who was to run TVA? President Roosevelt chose three directors. Writing in *Collier's Weekly* magazine in June 1934, Walter Davenport told of them and their assignment.

About a year ago two school teachers and a lawyer shook hands with President Roosevelt, told him how much they had enjoyed the luncheon, and took the next train to Knoxville, Tennessee. Collectively they were the Tennessee Valley Authority—directors of the Authority. They had been given fifty million dollars and told to look over the valley's 40,000 square miles of hills and forests, farms and cities, and draw up a plan of operation as rapidly as possible. For this they were each to get ten thousand dollars a year, plenty of personal authority and all the expert help they needed, the country being full of unemployed experts.

Separately the two school teachers are Mr. Arthur E. Morgan, President of Antioch College at Yellow Springs, Ohio; and Mr. Harcourt A. Morgan, formerly president of The University of Tennessee. The lawyer is Mr. David E. Lilienthal of Chicago . . .

The three directors would take charge of the corporation, which, in Roosevelt's words, was to be "clothed with the power of government but possessed of the flexibility and initiative of a private enterprise." The directors were fully accountable to the President and to Congress. Arthur Morgan, besides being a notable educator, had planned and built seventy-five water-control projects. Harcourt Morgan was an agricultural specialist and had an intimate knowledge of the South and its problems. David Lilienthal was a young lawyer with experience in public service.

On the construction front, these three men had to set in motion simultaneously two major operations. The first was to buy up the land needed for the project, evacuate the people whose farmlands would be buried under the waters of the new reservoirs, and clear the land for flooding. The second was to build all the dams and reservoirs.

It was a year after the signing of the act when reporter Walter Davenport went to the Tennessee valley to have a look for *Collier's*. His objective was to see how the valley's "two million inhabitants were taking to the most ambitious land-planning experiment America has ever undertaken." Construction was already under way on Norris Dam. Davenport described his discoveries:

First we stopped at Mitchell's Lunch Room in Loyston, Tennessee . . .

We were glad we stopped at Loyston, not merely because we met the Judge but because it was about our last chance. When the Tennessee Valley Authority has finished Norris Dam on the Clinch River about twenty

*This Loyston homestead—furnished with oil
lamps and spinning wheel—was in the region later
inundated by the waters of the Norris Dam reservoir.
The photograph is by Lewis Hine.*

miles northwest of Knoxville, there won't be any Loyston. It will be a couple of hundred feet under water. The Judge, who spends his days between Mitchell's Lunch Room and George Fox's garage, depending upon which side of the road strange cars stop, gave us his opinion that the result would be sensational only to the natives as nobody else in the world would know that Loyston had ever been anywhere anyway. And Loyston (population 100) won't be the only village that will be at the bottom of Norris Lake. Lead Mine Bend will be . . . and Goin too. And a couple more . . . Spitting expertly over his beard, the Judge continued, "At first when they told us Loyston was going to be under a couple hundred feet of water, we rose up. We said if they drowned Loyston they drowned us along with her. A man's home's his home. I ain't saying Loyston's anything to quit living in New York or Washington or Tupelo or any of those big cities for; but we got right used to Loyston and it never did us any harm. That's what we said."

"What changed your minds, Judge?"

"Some one thing and some another," he said. "With me, now, I'm an old man. If you keep going down this road a piece till you come to—well, anyway it's a graveyard. Lots of people around the hills here have got folks there. When you get old you look at things different. Well, that graveyard will be a hundred feet under water but there won't be anybody there. The government's moving those graves like it was Arlington Cemetery. Those and a lot more in graveyards where the water'll be. New headstones on high ground and not a spade hits the earth till the family's satisfied and all present with a preacher saying the prayer. The history of these hills is on those old gravestones, mister."

The Judge accepted a bottle of pop, holding down his beard while he fitted it nicely to his lips. "With some folks it was something else," he said. "For instance the government—these Authority people—set fair prices on farm land that will be under water, on farm land and buildings. We're simple people, maybe, but nobody with enough sense to keep out of the ditch is accusing us of being dumb. They asked us how much we'd take and we told them. Then we asked them how much they'd give and they told us. We split the difference."

Winning the confidence of the valley's people was the primary task of the directors. The *Collier's* article said,

It is wholly possible that much of the efforts of the TVA would have been mired forthwith and progress made many times as expensive, if not impossible, had the Authority failed to handle such human incidentals as the moving of those graves the Judge spoke about, with reverence and without haste . . .

Similarly, the Authority went about the moving of churches, repairing them, painting them, re-roofing them. Schools that had to be moved received similar gentle treatment and where farmers had doubts about where and when to move, the Authority lent them quiet aid. Thus the beginnings were accomplished, the most delicate beginnings, and rapidly the Authority won the Valley's common people.

But it was not always easy. Some of the mountaineers bitterly resented TVA's intrusion into their realm. A

ORVALINE
BELCHER,
APR. 3, 1868
FEB. 18, 1919

news article described the human side of the experiment at the end of the first year.

Chattanooga, Tenn. June 29, 1934. There is one discordant note in the symphony of expectation and hope to be heard in the Tennessee Valley today, a year after the government began its great economic and social experiment.

It comes from the hills and mountains and coves where dwell inhabitants who have never known the meaning of the word "progress." They are the mountaineers, famed in fiction and fact, who still live in rude log cabins, shoot squirrels and make their own corn liquor.

Down in the valley, in the cities and towns and in the farm-lands, there is a significant stirring. Proudly, confidently, they will tell you—the lowlanders—that the Tennessee Valley Authority is the biggest thing in their lives.

It is no wonder, for whether it succeeds or fails it is of tremendous importance to the entire nation. Officials sit in offices in Knoxville and in Washington, and issue statements of vast import. They say that this is the exhibit A of the country's future social and economic planning. They quote statistics which show that the Tennessee basin encompasses 40,000 square miles, touching seven states; that it affects the lives of 2,000,000 human beings while three times that number live within its sphere of influence.

But the man of the hills did not see eye to eye with all that "fancy talk"; he was suspicious:

To him the government consists of a President in a white shirt and a gang of nosy revenuers. He does not like government interference with his life, now or at any time. I sat on the stoop of a mountain cabin and heard a hillsman express that statement.

In him is the embodiment of one discouraging, almost desperate, problem facing the engineers, socio-economists and professional religionists who have come this way from Washington. They go about the country, or into the halls of Rotary Clubs or Chambers of Commerce in the cities, uttering large phrases about social reorganization, economic planning, land utilization, decentralization, soil erosion, afforestation, flood control and fertilizer distribution.

The hillsman puts two fingers to his mouth, spits out tobacco between them, then taps a forefinger to his forehead and exclaims: "Them guvment fellers are a little crazy."

Anyone who came around with pencil and paper in hand tended to be mistrusted—as this old Southern spiritual shows.

There's a Man Goin' 'Round Takin' Names

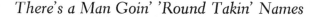

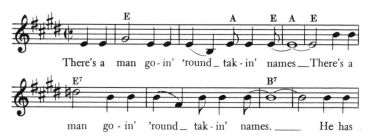

There's a man go-in' 'round_ tak-in' names __There's a man go-in' 'round_ tak-in' names. _____ He has

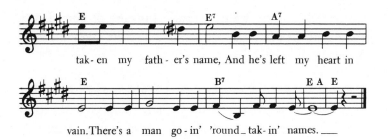

tak-en my fath-er's name, And he's left my heart in

vain. There's a man go-in' 'round_ tak-in' names. __

There's a man goin' 'round takin' names.
There's a man goin' 'round takin' names.
He has taken my mother's name
And has left me here in vain.
There's a man goin' 'round takin' names.

. . . He has taken my sister's name . . .
. . . He has taken my brother's name . . .

Words and music by Huddie Ledbetter; TRO © 1963, Folkways Music Publishers, Inc., New York, New York. Used by permission.

Meanwhile, "them guvment fellers" had hard decisions to make. The purchase of land, for example, was ticklish. It could not long remain a matter of splitting the difference between the TVA offer and the price set by the owner. One farmer might be a good trader, another a poor one. So it was decided to send field appraisers to estimate the value of each farm, with its timber and its improvements, and to make an offer. If the farmer refused the offer, the federal court appointed a local commission to review the evidence, talk to the owner, and make a ruling. If the farmer still rejected the offer, legal condemnation proceedings would follow—slowly. In a few instances a lawsuit had to settle the matter.

Inevitably there were a certain number of complaints about the prices paid for land. The Birmingham, Alabama, *Post* carried this story in 1934:

Decatur, Dec. 19. Charges and denials surged today over prices the Tennessee Valley Authority's land acquisition department has been paying to owners whose property will be flooded by the backwaters from Wheeler Dam.

Following organization of the Tennessee Valley Landowners Mutual Aid Agency, which charges the TVA department with paying unfair prices, dozens of prominent landowners have leaped to the defense of the Governmental unit with declarations that their dealings with it have been satisfactory.

The landowners' agency, headed by John W. Knight, Decatur real estate man, charged publicly that "Misstatements are being recklessly made to landowners to accelerate purchases and to close trades. This is manifestly unfair."

Among the landowners upholding TVA was Judge James Horton of Athens. "Some people think the TVA is Santa Claus," he said. "They wouldn't be satisfied with anything."

But there were beyond doubt cases of hardship and heartbreak. For the Douglas Dam reservoir on the French Broad, more than 30,000 acres of eastern Tennessee soil would have to be sacrificed. James Hoskins, president of the University of Tennessee, commented:

Good soil exists elsewhere, and for a price it may be had. When a home is destroyed, however, the loss may

*Late winter on a farm
in one of the mountain coves.*

be irretrievable . . . Farm homes thrust their roots deep within the soil . . .

What provision can be made for these dispossessed? Is a Government check or ready cash any solution to their problem? What wounds will this money heal? . . . There is more than damage here. There is destruction, irreparable destruction, irretrievable loss for some 3,000 persons.

This deep sense of loss applied particularly to older people who, for a lifetime, had called these farms, fields, and hills their home. To these folk, every building, every crossroads, had a priceless history. As Cherokee Dam was going up, an article in the Knoxville *News Sentinel* of August 25, 1940, said:

FINE HOMES AND OTHER LANDMARKS WILL
DISAPPEAR IN CHEROKEE DAM LAKE.

There are two faces to Cherokee Dam—the one looking forward into tomorrow, the other back on a yesterday that will be drowned.

Both are as American as tractors and log cabins, and both light up pictures in your mind . . .

At Bean Station, where your roadmaps mark the junction of Highways 32 and 11W, Cherokee Lake waters will blot out a famous crossroads of the wilderness, part of an old tavern which was the finest between Washington and New Orleans, several old homes nearby and many landmarks.

Its history of almost 200 years is summed up briefly on a marker placed by the D.A.R.

"This is one of the first settlements in Tennessee. William Bean and Daniel Boone camped near here about 1775. Indians massacred the first settlers, a family named English. Permanently settled by William II, George and Jesse Bean who were granted over 3000 acres of land along German Creek for Revolutionary services.

"A fort was erected in 1787 for protection from the Indians. William II and Robert Bean being captains of militia. The Bean house located 70 feet from this marker formed one corner of the fort and was built over a spring to insure water for defendants in case of siege.

"Here was the intersection of Daniel Boone's Trail and the Great Warpath of the Cherokee, later a cross-roads of Baltimore to Nashville stage road and Kentucky and Carolina turnpike."

"They say that the water will be 12 feet over the cemetery," said Mrs. Jessie Gill Williams, postmistress of Bean Station. "The graves will be moved. It's like the end of the world. We thought we could sympathize with the people at Norris Dam, but we couldn't until now."

Her big brick house, built to last out time, must go. Its walls are 18 inches thick, its partitions of solid brick, the curved stairway, the mantels, the ceiling of its living room all woodwork handcarved.

Her grandfather, Samuel Gill, had it built by Jabe Cooley, a master builder of early Tennessee. Five years in the building, nothing but the best bricks that could be made and the strongest timbers were good enough.

Samuel Gill raised 16 children here. It has been home to four generations of the family. Around it stretch 500 acres of rich farm land.

It is natural to ask whether or not it could be moved.

"My house is built so strong they will have to dynamite it," Mrs. Williams said.

There was a horror in the quiet way she said it that could have been no greater than if she faced bombs dropping out of the sky.

Equally distressed were many of the old people who lived in tumble-down mountain cabins on steep, washed-out land. One writer, Katherine Glover, visited a hilly section in the eastern valley in the late 1930s. Construction was already under way on Hiwassee Dam nearby.

It is early summer . . . We stop at one of the native cabins of weathered logs and mortar, half tumbling on its foundations, and yet, like the people of these hills, retaining the dignity of a primitive grace.

Beside the cabin are steep hills, for the most part stripped and bare. One is planted to corn, and two women are at work hoeing between the stalks . . .

On the porch of the cabin is an old woman, plain, rugged, worn thin with work and much living. "Granny Forbes," as the natives call her, will be among those who will be moving to make way for this new world that is building. When the valley of the Hiwassee is flooded for the reservoir, she and her daughter and her daughter's children and their neighbors, who are the very bone and sinew of these hills, will be finding new homes.

When she is asked how she feels about leaving, she gives a sharp look through her steel spectacles, dropped low on her thin, finely shaped nose: "Same's you would, I reckon, if you'd seen the sun a-risin' and a-settin' over these mountains nigh on eighty year', and yer mammy and yer pappy and yer gran'pappy before yer. It'll rise and set, I reckon, the same on yon side the ridge where we'll be a-goin', but 'twon't never look the same."

She shifts in her chair. "The young'uns mebbe'll sprout in new earth, but I'm too old fer sproutin' " . . .

"Aunt Sally" Boober, aged ninety-five, had a different way of looking at things. She viewed the necessary move from Big Creek on the Holston with equanimity and even with a measure of anticipation: "I could have gone from here long ago but I stuck to my home. But wherever I go, there'll be good people and good things to do." As she talked she sat straight in a rocking chair, her hand clutching a walking stick. She sat before a large open fireplace in the living room of her six-room log and frame home.

"My husband Peter fought for the South in the Civil War and when he came back we had a hard time rearing our six children from the soil here," she said. "But I've always said that no matter what happened there was a way out for me. I'll not worry. Worrying over what they can't help kills people."

A number of the evacuees found that they had actually bettered themselves by moving. The *News Sentinel* of Knoxville gave an example:

One man in Swain County owned several hundred acres scattered around in little patches . . . TVA bought all of his property except one tract. He took the money and went over toward Gateway. There he bought a nice

75-acre farm, comparatively level, and heavy farm machinery.

He always had an ambition to raise stock. Now he can cultivate crops, raise grain and cattle. He received enough from his four or five tracts of scattered rough land to buy the new farm, with a substantial amount of money left to realize his old hope of stocking a farm with purebred cattle.

The evacuating had to go on and on, year after year, to provide space for the waterholding reservoirs behind the new dams. There were nine on the Tennessee itself and some two dozen on its tributaries—the Clinch, the Holston, the French Broad, the Little Tennessee, the Hiwassee.

No one could "stay put" no matter what his or her feelings, no matter how hard the moving, especially from the mountain coves. The Knoxville *News Sentinel* told this story:

Some of those who lived deep in the mountains have never been far from home. For instance, there is an old woman who lives back in the Proctor area (of North Carolina) two miles up in a cove, where it is impossible to take a car. She is rather feeble. Mr. W. T. Hunt (in charge of TVA's population readjustment program) was talking to one of her sons not long ago.

"I impressed on him the necessity for getting out of the cove while the weather is good," said Mr. Hunt. "He told me that his mother had not been to Proctor in 30 years and had never been to Bryson City, about 25 miles away. She had never been in an automobile."

Blasting for Cherokee Dam, 1941.

Some families use a sled, pulled by an ox, to haul belongings out of coves.

As the people left family by family, the reservoir clearance crew went to work. A description of the "trail of desolation" left by the wreckers once they started "destroying everything in their wake" is found in this account from the *Towns County Herald* of Hiawassee, Georgia:

Wildlife was on the run from the 4,560 acres of timber land being cleared. Many quail were easy marks for the hunters as they left the woods seeking new homes. The rabbits that escaped will prey upon nearby farms and orchards.

We got our share of fleeing mice and rats as the barns and cribs were torn down.

The destruction of all that fine timber was not good to see.

The area now has the appearance of a country struck by a tornado. Debris, a few shrubs broken down by the house-movers, a lone chimney speak of the day when a family lived here. A family who worked and hoped and loved.

A hen was left. She looked forlorn as she tried to cross the muddy road in search of a roosting place that was there no more. Will she wander to the forest ahead of the waters, and there go wild?

The roads are all torn up, and muddy. The hillsides are scarred and bare.

In all, TVA's five-state construction program, which neared completion in 1944, inundated 610,000 acres of land and evacuated some 13,500 families from the valley.

☆ 5 ☆

"THEY'LL BUILD THAT DAM
OR BUST"

The hills resounded to the blasting and the drilling. One giant dam and then another rose from the riverbed as the countryside was cleared to receive the waters of the "new" river. It was a major engineering task. How, asked the engineers, can a waterway best be harnessed to provide at one and the same time smooth navigation, flood control, and hopefully also the generation of electricity?

Smooth navigation demanded a nine-foot depth of channel water at all seasons. There had to be dams. And there had to be a series of locks—the fewer the better—to raise and lower boats past the dams.

Flood control required huge reservoirs to catch and hold water. During flood season itself, the water level in the reservoirs would have to be kept low, ready to retain runoff.

But the efficient generation of electricity required just the opposite—reservoirs as full as possible. The larger the head of water that spins the turbines (which, in turn, spin the generators), the more hydropower. Obviously, high dams with full reservoirs behind them would give the best electric potential for the generators.

Many engineers throughout the country believed it impossible for one dam system to meet all these objectives. Some believed it could be done. These men were sought and found and invited to join the staff of TVA.

There were two possible alternatives for construction —a string of thirty-two low dams or a series of nine high dams. Low dams would be cheaper but would have no value for flood control. High dams would control floods, generate more electricity, and require fewer locks. The issue was decided in favor of high dams.

To reconcile flood control (relatively empty reservoirs) with high power potential (full reservoirs), two different types of dams were constructed. On the tributaries, TVA decided to build very high dams with deep reservoirs for storing flood waters. There were to be powerhouses but no locks. The mainstream dams would primarily even out the nine-foot channel, rather than stop floods. They would be long, massive dams, generally quite a bit lower than those on the tributaries. There would be locks for boats navigating the channel. And some powerhouses, though, because the reservoirs behind them would store less water, they would give less electric potential than the powerhouses on the tributaries.

Now the business of dam building began. It required a veritable army of workers. Recruiting was no real problem, however, for during the great depression thousands on thousands of people in the valley were in dire need of work. The problem was who to hire from among all the unemployed.

A merit system was devised and general examinations

were held to test ability to follow written and oral instructions. Only those who had first filed the famous "Form 10 TVA" blank were eligible.

In the fall of 1933 two examinations were held in 138 centers. Men came from Tennessee and parts of Kentucky, Virginia, North Carolina, Alabama, Georgia, and Mississippi. Gordon Clapp, associated with TVA from the beginning and later chairman of the board, described them:

> The thousands of men from farms and cities, from mountain coves and cotton-gin towns, who assembled, pencil in hand, on those two December days in 1933 were probably unaware that they were making history in a method for the recruitment and selection of a labor force. Their presence in the post-office rooms, schoolhouses, and churches which served as examination centers was a public demonstration of a new approach to construction work . . . They were men who had decided to assemble for this strange kind of examination instead of relying on the assurance of harassed political captains that a job would be obtained for the party faithfuls without going through special procedures . . . For many thousands of men this was a gamble. They might lose, and those who relied on patronage might win . . .

Almost 39,000 men presented themselves for the first examination and 98,000 for the second, two years later. Skilled, semiskilled, and unskilled workmen were hired. The merit system worked well—unusually so, some thought, for the quarter of a million Negroes living in the Tennessee valley. A white Southerner, writing in the

A TVA interviewer talks to job applicants
at a country store in Lead Mine Bend,
Tennessee, 1933. Photo by Hine.

Negro magazine *Opportunity,* commented in a 1934 issue:

As a relief measure or job providing agency, which it really does not purport to be, the TVA has dealt with the Negro more justly than possibly any other one of the New Deal Acts. Certainly more than the NRA [National Recovery Act] for example, which in most cases in the South has either not been applied at all to Negroes or else has simply been the occasion to throw them completely out of work. TVA authorities claim, and I have no facts with which to dispute such claims, that they are employing Negroes according to their proportion of the total population and in all cases paying them the same wages that whites received for doing the same work. In the building of the Joe Wheeler Dam, for example, that more than a mile-long structure being erected fifteen and a half miles above Muscle Shoals, the 523 men now employed are, according to the TVA Personnel Division, divided between the races according to their proportionate population in the territory from which the labor is being drawn. The wage scale of 45¢ for unskilled and $1.00 for skilled labor is, according to the same authority, being applied to all regardless of color. Likewise, in the Norris project, twenty miles northwest of Knoxville, among the total number of workers now on the payroll some 7 per cent are Negroes which is about their proportion of the population in the twelve counties surrounding Norris.

Another Negro paper, *Crisis,* dissented and gave these reasons:

For the most part skilled work is denied Negro workers. Employment of labor is done through the TVA personnel division. Negro workers are employed by Negro assistant personnel officers under the supervision of white officials. To the Negro assistants only requisitions for unskilled work is given. Thus the assistants cannot offer skilled work to any Negro applicants. Only by currying favor with white bosses, may a Negro worker once on the job hope to rise to a higher level of pay or skilled employment. Such instances are very few.

But the same article concluded that discrimination was not so much a TVA problem as a problem of the South in its entirety.

For those people in the valley, black or white, who got jobs, and particularly for the young—those who in Granny Forbes's words could still "sprout"—the coming of TVA meant a new start and the promise of a future with more than a glimmer of hope in it. These feelings were expressed in an exuberant ballad:

The TVA Song

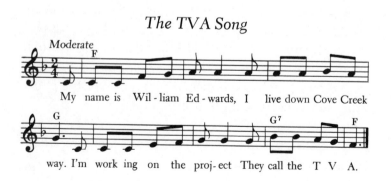

My name is Wil-liam Ed-wards, I live down Cove Creek way. I'm work ing on the proj-ect They call the T V A.

The Government begun it
When I was but a child;
But now they are in earnest,
And Tennessee's gone wild.

Just see them boys a-comin',
Their tool kits on their arm;
They come from Clinch and Holston
And many a valley farm.

From villages and cities,
A French Broad man I see;
For things are up and doing
In sunny Tennessee.

All up and down the valley
They heard the glad alarm,
"The Government means business!"
It's working like a charm.

Oh, see them boys a-comin',
Their Government they trust;
Just hear their hammers ringing,
They'll build that dam or bust.

Oh, things looked blue and lonely
Until this come along;
Now hear the crew a-singin'
And listen to their song.

"The Government employs us,
Short hours and certain pay;
Oh things are up and comin',
God bless the TVA."

Many of these young men came straight from the farm with no skill to recommend them except perhaps the knack of keeping a beat-up jalopy in running order. They acquired new skills directly on the job.

Norris Dam was the first dam TVA built. Ross White, who supervised the construction, told the Chattanooga *Times* of June 3, 1934, how a dam goes up:

Normal masonry dam construction usually calls for four major operations. They are:

1. River diversion.
2. Stripping and preparing foundations.
3. Producing and transporting concrete aggregates.
4. Mixing and placing concrete.

Many other features, such as access roads, construction camp, grouting of foundation, reservoir clearing, relocation of roads and railroads, etc., take on more or less importance in individual cases, but the four features mentioned will, in general, control the selection of construction plant and methods.

Norris Dam is no exception to this rule.

The *Nashville Tennessean* of August 10, 1934, gave a visitor's impressions of the dam site:

A bee-hive of activity awaits the visitor at Norris Dam. A battalion working in squads, husky men with sledges and power drills ripping up the hillsides, cave men funneling in the face of a cliff, youngsters spraying water on the green concrete, cranes hoisting scale-pans full of dirt and rock to a waiting truck a hundred feet above the power-house pit, mighty shovels whirling for a crunching bite in a rock pile and over all a distant hum and clang

*A Wheeler Dam workman
with his pneumatic drill.*

mingles with the intermittent grinding of nearby gears. Above the hundred noises comes a series of shrill, warning whistles, workers in the danger zone scamper to cover, a heavy explosion wakes the valley echoes, a mountain side crashes and the general din again announces that all is well.

Hundreds of feet overhead spectacular cableways span the valley. A bucket as big as a coal truck looms down from the sky filled with 12 tons of concrete. Guided by unseen hands it settles down among a group of puddlers as gently as a feather falls from a flying bird.

Work shifts at Norris were five and a half hours long. There were four shifts a day, to give more unemployed, depression-weary men a chance to work.

Another visitor to Norris Dam observed the enormous physical dangers involved in the building of a dam. *National Safety News* of November 1935 carried this article:

When you have electricians, riggers, mechanics, quarrymen, woodsmen, drillers, grouters, carpenters, concrete layers, and a host of laborers engaged in their various hazardous jobs throughout a mountainous, backward region 80 miles from tip to tip, you have a safety job on your hands . . .

The dam itself will reach slightly less than 2000 feet between two hills. It is being poured in sections or blocks of solid concrete which stretch 48 in line across the valley . . .

As the blocks are poured, the electricians, carpenters, concrete workers, engineers, and others must climb on ladders located on the down-river face to reach the pouring level. Since this face measures more than 200 feet in height as the block nears completion, a slip would result in almost certain death. The workman would roll and pitch down the steep side to the base of the dam or a baffle platform full of debris below.

As the height of the dams increased, the problem of safety on the ladders became more and more serious. And so

The sections of the long ladders on the down stream face of the dam are now staggered and are equipped with substantial platforms placed at approximately 50 foot intervals. These platforms not only provide a resting place for the men passing up and down but would, in the event of a fall, tend to reduce its seriousness. At quitting time when the ladders are full, a man at the top with a heavy kit of tools on his shoulder could fall and knock from the ladder many of the men below him. Staggering the ladders reduces the number of men endangered.

Safety education kept pace with safety devices. But safety education was only one among many educational programs available to the construction gang. Director Arthur Morgan described a visit to the men in their off-hours:

Last night I visited the workmen at the Norris Dam. The day's work was over for two of the four shifts . . . Some of the men were loafing in the bunk houses or dormitories, whichever we may choose to call them. Some were asleep, to be called for the midnight shift. Perhaps three hundred were having an old-time singing-bee in the mess house. Whoever heard of that in a construction gang? Over half of them have registered voluntarily for a share in the training program, which will help to turn them from laborers lucky to get a job, into effectively trained men, ready to take the results of a land-use survey and to dig out careers for themselves. Never in my engineering career have I seen such a clean-cut, intelligent and purposeful labor gang . . . The credit union (cooperative bank) in one end of the mess hall was crowded with men cashing checks, making deposits and taking out memberships. All these men want is a job, some training, some guidance . . .

The training program consisted of classes in agriculture, trades, engineering, natural science, mathematics, history, current events—and even music appreciation.

As for recreation, the Knoxville *News Sentinel* reported in late summer of 1934:

When the day's work is done at Norris Dam, the play begins at the construction camp.

There are two ping pong tables in the lobby of the Community Building and this form of "indoor tennis" is very popular at night when the outdoor variety can't be played.

Boxing is always a popular sport when red-blooded young men get together, and the TVA camp is no exception.

Shuffle board is another game to the liking of the TVA workers. As a rule you have to board an ocean liner to play this game, but there are two shuffle board courts in the Community Building.

Outdoor sports consist of baseball, tennis, horseback riding and horseshoe pitching.

In addition, there are movies and dances at night. The workers have their own orchestra for dancing, and an amateur dramatic club.

There were women at work, too, office and cafeteria workers among them. A Knoxville girl, who had a stenographer's job at Norris Dam, described her move to the newly planned "model" town of Norris:

I left Knoxville in its blanket of smoke and came to a place where there was fresh air, and the fragrance of pine trees, and the eternal serenity of the hills. It was peace after tumult, order after chaos, beauty after ugliness. And yet I have had dozens of people say to me, "How can you live in Norris?" . . .

When I came to Norris, I had the phrases all down pat. A permanent, planned community. Electrically equipped houses. A modern school, a demonstration farm and dairy, an up-to-date drug store. A trade shop, a library, and a recreation building for workers. Design in living. So often had I heard the glib words "model town" that it was somewhat of a jolt to find that after all I was living in a construction camp!

The first shock came when I saw my room in the great wooden barracks which housed the feminine contingent of Norris. A tiny room, the size of a matchbox. Rough pine walls, an iron cot, a table, a cane-bottomed chair. Nothing else.

The first day I thought, "Is it possible that this can

house a human soul?" The second day I discovered that fifty-eight human souls were bearing up remarkably under the circumstances and managing, moreover, to retain their identity. The third day I had decided that the room was adorable, but needed fixing up.

When I think now of that room in Barracks 7, which no longer exists, I want to laugh and weep. It was so rough and lovely and incongruous . . .

The second jolt was the matter of meals. It was not so much a question of being nourished as a question of how to keep from being over-nourished. The cuisine at Norris cafeteria is of a kind to sustain manual labor. We dine at long wooden benches, among overall-ed working men who stare at us with a kind of dumb wonder. Picking at our mountains of mashed potatoes and chunks of corn bread and slabs of apple pie, and sipping our muddy coffee out of great thick mugs, we stare back, solemn-eyed. The wonder is friendly and mutual.

But once bed and board were disposed of, she wrote,

I am free to revel in my small and thrilling part in this tremendous project in the Tennessee Valley. For seven hours a day I work busily at letters and memoranda, and shorthand and typing, and filing and telephoning and map-coloring. Somehow I feel that these humble hurry-ings and scurryings have a direct and significant part in the program of the Authority—the dam-building and flood control, the soil conservation and power generation, the social and economic betterment.

For when I close my eyes, shutting out the typewriter and the wall-maps and the filing cases, I see the starved faces of the hill people, to whom this experiment is endeavoring to bring a richer and a fuller life.

High spirits were everywhere in evidence at the dam site. Labor and management cooperated to an almost unprecedented degree. Architect John Kyle observed that

there was a continued flow of ideas and information back and forth at every level—from the drafting rooms to the tool sheds—for the same spirit permeating the architectural and engineering divisions of TVA was felt by the truck drivers and the work gangs, by the foremen and the timekeepers.

For him, the physical prospect of the dams, too, generated excitement. He wrote:

Dams, however, large or small, are always fascinating, but in 1936 Norris Dam, TVA's first, attracted attention out of its importance in flood control and power generation. Its forcefulness and simplicity held an extraordinary appeal for architects, engineers, and laymen alike. Critics uninterested in politics waxed enthusiastic about it; artists came to portray its sculptural quality; photographers came to study its lights and shadows, its textures and planes.

Norris was only the first in the series of dams that rose in the Tennessee River basin. An overall impressionistic view of how the dam-building process looked to a layman traveling from site to site is given by author R. L. Duffus:

He [the visitor] will remember driving through the mud to get to the Guntersville site when the first cofferdam [a temporary dam thrown around a construction area to clear it of water] was beginning to take shape. How could form come out of that chaos?

He will remember the shovels wrestling with the earth down in the cofferdam at Pickwick. What would happen if the rising river topped the dam? We'd have warning, says the engineer; we'd take them out in time. If the coffer washed out—we'd build it again.

He will remember the littered landscape at Chickamauga, and how his guide seemed to see as plainly as though it were there, each form and angle of the completed structure; and how he came back, and they were there.

He will remember the man cutting hay in what was soon to be the bottom of the Cherokee reservoir, and how the little farm and the house among the trees seemed as though they were to be there forever—but they weren't.

He will remember the awesome tunnels and scraped cliffs at Fontana and how impossible it was that a river in this setting could ever be controlled—but it was destined to be, and the engineers never had the least doubt about it.

As the dams were completed, the construction workers from the valley must have feared that they would fall back into the old life of poor crops and uncertain income. They wrote a song about leaving the dam sites called "This Ole Job." Here is one chorus:

Ain't a-gon na need this badge no long er,
Ain't a-gon na use this badge much more,
Ain't got time to stop and lin-ger, Ain't got time to
close the door, Ain't got time to ask for rais-es,
I don't want to start no row, Like the oth-ers
I'll be leav-ing, I'm get-ting rea-dy to job-hunt now.

Job hunting there would have to be; nevertheless, as the men returned to their hillside farms, they must have taken home with them memories of the dam-building experience. Perhaps some of their habitual fatalism was tempered now with a sense of hope.

Considering the first twenty years of TVA's accomplishments in building dams to harness the river, Gordon Clapp estimated that

Construction work in progress
at Fort Loudon Dam, 1942.

These dams represent more than one-half billion dollars. One hundred and thirteen million cubic yards of concrete, rock, and earth fill, twelve times the bulk of the seven great pyramids of Egypt, have been used to build these structures into the river bed of the Tennessee and its tributaries. Almost two hundred thousand different men and women at one time or another have been employed by TVA for a direct part in the colossal job.

"Money, materials, machines and men" he concluded, "are the basic ingredients in building a dam. And," he added, "the greatest of these is men."

☆ ⑥ ☆

TURNING OFF THE RIVER
LIKE A SPIGOT

The work of creating a new river from the shallow, turbulent, and flood-menaced Tennessee took a full ten years. One by one the nine giant dams were constructed. From east to west, from source to mouth, they were Fort Loudoun, Watts Bar, Chickamauga, Nickajack, Guntersville, Wheeler, Wilson, Pickwick, and Kentucky. When Kentucky Dam was completed in 1944, TVA finished its dam building on the mainstream of the Tennessee. Then there were the chief dams and reservoirs on the tributary rivers—Norris on the Clinch, Cherokee on the Holston, Douglas on the French Broad, Fontana on the Little Tennessee, Hiwassee on the Hiwassee.

One observer likened the series of dams to the military strategy of defense in depth. The first line of defense is the system of nine great dams and reservoirs on the mainstream. They are backed up by the five high dams and basins on the tributary rivers. These are the structures designed primarily for flood control. Finally, there are the mountain reservoirs that catch and hold part of the huge tonnage of potential flood water.

And how did this elaborate flood-control system actually work? Let us imagine that it is the time of heavy rains. The pamphlet *TVA Tames a River* describes a day during flood season:

At 7:30 each morning in the TVA River Control Branch at Knoxville, a facsimile machine begins to whine as it reproduces sheets placed on a similar machine in the Office of Power in Chattanooga—sheets filled with data on rainfall, reservoir elevations, and discharges at each TVA dam.

Then a teletype begins to click out the weather forecast from the U.S. Weather Bureau at Knoxville airport . . .

At 8:00 the telephones ring, and for the next thirty minutes a steady stream of information pours in from 200 rainfall stations and 50 stream gauges scattered through the Valley . . .

At 9:15 preliminary estimates of TVA's expected operation at Kentucky Dam—which will affect the lower Ohio and Mississippi Rivers—are sent to the Corps of Engineers at Cincinnati and the U.S. Weather Bureau at Cairo. In return TVA gets observed stages and flows on these rivers.

If the rainfall and streamflow reports are ominous, water already in the Tennessee River must be rushed down stream to make room for a possible flood. Orders are given to the Office of Power for operations at the dams: Increase Watts Bar discharge 20,000, Guntersville and Wheeler 25,000 and Pickwick and Kentucky 40,000 . . .

Meanwhile all the rainfall and streamflow data are trans-

The Norris Dam spillway.

mitted to TVA's big computer in Chattanooga, which quickly converts that mass of figures into predictions of the amount of water which will be flowing into each of 39 reservoirs . . .

Armed with this vital information, the key engineers go into a huddle. They must decide how much of the inflow into each reservoir should be stored and how much released . . . These decisions must be made quickly—but they must be right.

Reservoir elevations and discharge are determined for the next several days and are relayed to the dams. Flood warnings are issued.

Calls begin to come in from people affected by the flood.

Industries at Chattanooga ask how long they will have to remove pumps and equipment. A tow approaching one of the locks can get through with the existing discharge but not if there is any increase—can the increase be delayed for an hour? . . .

A farmer below Guntersville Dam has 50 pigs on an island. Another one foot rise will drown them. Can TVA stop further increases until they are removed? . . .

Next morning at 7:30 the sequence starts again—and on the following morning, and the next. The crest is passed at Chattanooga, and the stage begins to drop. Gate discharge is started at the tributary dams to draw out the excess water stored during the flood.

Now the flood wave is nearing big Kentucky Reservoir, linked with the [Army] Corps' Barkley Reservoir on the Cumberland to form a vast storage combination on the lower reaches of these two major rivers. Far to the north, the Ohio River also is swollen with rain . . . As the Ohio crest approaches, part—or even all—of the flow of the Tennessee and Cumberland Rivers is held out of the Ohio River flood.

Gradually flows recede and the excess water which has been stored is passed on down the Ohio and the Mississippi. The TVA system is back to normal, ready for the next flood.

The flood danger season begins in late December, for rainfall in the Tennessee valley is usually heaviest around the first of the year. But more critical as far as floods are concerned is the fact that the rainwater running off into the streams is always greatest in winter, after the crops have been harvested. The trees are dormant then, and transpiration—the evaporation of moisture from green plants into the air—is at a minimum. In these circumstances, the ground becomes so quickly saturated that the rain, instead of being soaked up, runs off into the streams and rivers. So the period from the first of the year to springtime, when the transpiration provided by crops and trees is under way again, is flood season.

Preparing for flood season, the engineers devised a year-around cycle of water control in the reservoirs. They explained:

The normal operation of the TVA system requires that all reservoirs be drawn down to low levels around January first of each year. This provides the greatest amount of empty space behind the dams to store the rains to come. As the rains are stored, water levels are allowed to rise

*This diagram explains how power is generated at a dam.
Water flows in (right), spins the turbine (center), and then
flows downstream (left). The revolving turbine spins the generator
(upper center) which produces electricity to be transmitted
to the countryside through the power lines (upper left).*

gradually until the flood season is over. In the fall, the draw-down [emptying] of the lakes begins again, once more providing for maximum flood storage by January first.

Protection against flooding has had enormous impact on the valley. The flood-protection system completely eliminates damages from floods as great as the maximum known on about 109,000 acres of Tennessee valley land.

Chattanooga, in the main Tennessee River valley, is subject to greater damage from flood than any other city in the region. In February 1957 there was a twenty-day storm that in former times would have caused the Tennessee to rise within four feet of the height of the 1867 flood. What actually happened was told by the *Times* of Huntsville, Alabama:

Knoxville, Tenn. Feb. 2 (AP). The Weather Bureau and Tennessee Valley Authority [have] concluded that Chattanooga would have been under 22 feet of water late Monday had it not been for TVA's system of dams . . .

TVA's chief water control engineer estimated that, but for the flood protection, damages of about 50 million dollars would have occurred.

The TVA dam system also aids in holding floods below the tops of levees protecting more than 6 million acres of productive land along the Mississippi River. The May 1, 1960, Florence, Alabama, *Times* cheered when

TVA TURNS OFF THE RIVER LIKE SPIGOT IN KITCHEN

Regulation of the Tennessee River during the Ohio–Mississippi River flood in April reduced the stage at

Cairo, Ill., an estimated 2.7 feet, saving an estimated $4,500,000 in damages on the lower Mississippi River, TVA reports. During the most critical period the entire flow of the Tennessee River system was completely shut off for three days at Kentucky Dam.

Each passing year adds its evidence of successful flood control. In March 1967 the magazine *The Engineer* reported:

The TVA system was operated to reduce three flood crests during the year, one at Chattanooga, Tennessee, and downstream points, and two on the Ohio and Mississippi. Approximately 1,500,000 dollars in flood damages were averted.

But no dollars-and-cents report can possibly estimate the heartbreak of sudden homelessness, the grief over lives that would have been lost had there been no protecting dams and reservoirs.

Turning off the flow of a river like a kitchen spigot was an incredible engineering feat. TVA impounded an entire river system behind dams. Quiet, slow-moving streams replaced turbulent ones. The mainstream became a series of quiet lakes—the reservoirs. As a side effect, however, a grave public health problem might have been in the offing: the larvae of the malaria-carrying mosquito are known to thrive in permanently ponded water and to feed on floating vegetation.

TVA experts—medical malariologists, entomologists, biologists, and engineers—set to work.

The most effective single control measure proved to

be changing the water level of the reservoirs. In mosquito-breeding season—spring and summer—the level of the water is lowered rapidly. The mosquito larvae are left stranded on the shoreline, where they die. Or the sudden movement of the water may dislodge them from floating material, leaving the larvae at the mercy of their natural enemies.

In addition, the shorelines of ponds were cleared of all vegetation that might encourage larval growth. Swampy areas were drained and larvicides were used. Malaria control, though a peripheral aspect of river control, proved a boon to the people of the valley, for malaria had been a common and debilitating disease throughout the South.

Of equal importance with flood control was the improvement of navigation on the river. The nine-foot channel was no mean engineering feat, for when TVA began, the river was unbelievably shallow in certain spots. The minimum depth below Sheffield, Alabama, was only four feet; between the head of Wilson Dam pool and Chattanooga, three feet; and between Chattanooga and Knoxville, only one foot.

"The Tennessee is to flow down a giant stairway from one end of the valley to the other," declared a TVA engineer. And this, in a manner of speaking, is what happened. The huge locks circumventing the nine mainstream dams made the 650-mile-long river, with a drop of 815 feet from top to bottom, a gentle, smooth-flowing stream.

What is it like for a boat or barge to drop from one

_The Tennessee River now flows
down a giant stairway._

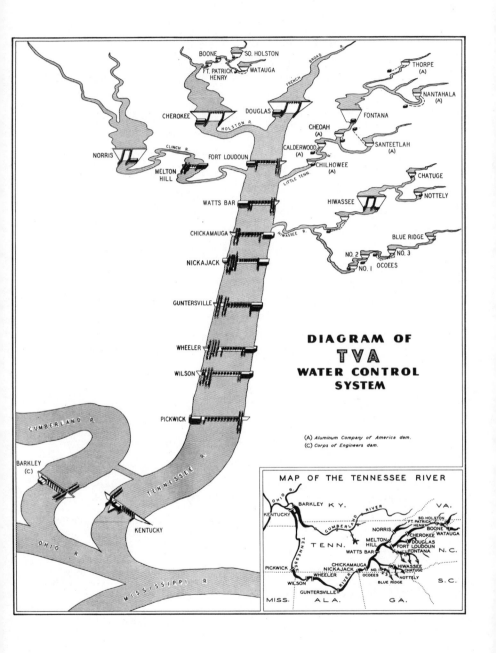

DIAGRAM OF
TVA
WATER CONTROL
SYSTEM

(A) *Aluminum Company of America dam.*
(C) *Corps of Engineers dam.*

MAP OF THE TENNESSEE RIVER

water level to another, from one step on the giant stair-way to the one next below?

As the boat glides into one of these locks [wrote Henry Billings in All Down the Valley] *and the upstream gates are silently closed by the electric motors that operate them, one has the feeling of sitting in a rowboat in a bathtub. Then, as the water drops, the walls seem to rise above the deck, the landscape disappears, and in a few minutes, you have dropped to the bottom of a huge rectangular well, whose dripping concrete walls rise 70 feet directly overhead to the little patch of blue sky. Then the downstream gates open majestically and there, stretching ahead as far as you can see, is another placid lake.*

One of the immediate changes on the new-old river was the improvement in shipping. In 1941 director David Lilienthal wrote:

I have just had a report on navigation: navigation, the stepchild and laughing stock, is going along as it has never done on any other river in America. For example, assembled automobiles, shipped as an experiment a few months ago, are now to be shipped on the river in large quantities, a shipment every other day. Not even on the famous channels of Europe has anything like that happened . . .

In 1955 Gordon Clapp wrote that new traffic records were being set regularly on the 630-mile navigation channel.

In the past year the new channel carried more than a billion ton-miles of freight. This was an increase of more than thirty-fold compared with river traffic before TVA began to improve the river. Formerly, the major traffic consisted of sand and gravel dredged from the river bed and hauled short distances and of forest products moved by barge. Now the modernized river—a chain of lakes joined together by single-lift locks—carries products of higher value, such as coal, oil, grain, and steel, and for longer distances, frequently between the Valley and the Middle West.

Ten years later, in the mid-1960's, over 17 million tons were carried on the river every year and the hauls were longer. The total in ton-miles was more than 2 billion— 70 times what it had been in 1933. The new shipping offered employment to more than 31,000 of the valley's workers.

Some of those in the valley must have been astonished by the newfangled, modern craft they saw gliding up and down the river. E. P. Ericson, a TVA staff member, described them in his book *TVA—The First Twenty Years*:

The old stern-wheel packet steamer has given way to an unromantic but highly efficient all-welded steel boat, its screw propellers driven by two or three Diesel engines totalling perhaps 5,000 horse power, pushing a fleet of steel barges carrying 20,000 tons of cargo or more—the equivalent of 400 rail carloads. The modern river queen is modern indeed, from radar for navigation through fogs to television for entertainment of the crew. It knows *little of the excitement that historians record for its fore-runner: it has seldom been stuck on a sand bank; it is kept in the channel by frequent buoys and lights; and it ties up at well-kept and well-attended terminals. But it plays an increasingly important part in America's industrial life, for river transportation in our day is big business.*

The transformation of the turbulent, treacherous river into a series of clear, unruffled lakes brought important fringe benefits too. For people to survive in a depressed region, they must work unremittingly with little or nothing to show for their labors. To prosper means in part to have the chance to play. Now, with the new navigable river, there came undreamed-of opportunities for recreation—nature to appreciate and enjoy rather than exploit. The waters of the Tennessee are now used for every kind of pleasure boating—tourist cruises, outboards, yachts, sailboats, fishing boats, houseboats, and canoes. On the tributaries—the Nolichucky, the French Broad, the Pigeon, the Little Tennessee—there are both smooth waters, and the rapids and falls loved by white-water canoeing enthusiasts. Many vacationers come from outside the region to the "Great Lakes of the South" to share in the pleasures provided by sparkling waters and unbroken miles of wooded shoreline.

Even steamships were to have their day again—now as tourist boats navigating the new placid lakes. An article in *The Waterways Journal* as early as 1942 announced that the tourist steamer *Gordon C. Greene* "departed from New Orleans for Cincinnati on May 19 with a cabin full of passengers all having a royal time." The ship was headed for Chattanooga "with something over 100 passengers enjoying the delights of river travel in the 1942 de luxe fashion on this 'first voyage' " up the Tennessee as far as the Alabama city.

A passenger on this steamer's return trip was Professor Donald Davidson of Vanderbilt University in Nashville. He kept his own personal ship's log and called it "Journal of a Voyage from Chattanooga to Paducah on the Good Steamboat *Gordon C. Greene.*"

June 6, 1942. We cast off at five o'clock in the morning . . . At first real daylight we are rounding Moccasin Bend. The river here is not too wide to imagine how it happened that Mr. Payne, of the Donelson party, was killed by an Indian's rifle, firing from the thickets . . . The Tennessee is smooth as glass, and you would never know that we are sliding over what used to be the Tumbling Shoals, a boulder-strewn, tumultous stretch; hardly anybody even remembers the name, these days . . .

It is good daylight when we steam toward the entrance of the Suck . . . The perfectly quiet water, unrippled except by our passage, reflects in reverse order the layered over-lapping bulk of the mountain walls . . .

We are entering the Great Bend of the Tennessee and the corn and cotton lands of North Alabama.

We are in the region of the permanent flood by which the TVA intends to prevent occasional floods, as well as achieve other multiple purposes. Here the Tennessee is no longer a river, but an inland sea lapping the distant ridges . . .

We are getting into the real lake now, above Guntersville . . . Here was probably the Indian town of Coste, where De Soto's men, marauding foolishly, almost got into a battle; and on McKee Island was the Tali, the main town of the Indian province, near which De Soto camped . . .

And on the west side the river-lake also surrounds Guntersville. It has new docks, and a boat harbor, but is no more just a river town, it looks more like a seaport . . .

The second day's journey took the *Gordon C. Greene* through the most notorious of all the Tennessee's old obstructions:

June 7, 1942. We lock through Wheeler Dam. Beyond is the famous region of Big Muscle Shoals, but it's just Wilson Lake now, and no excitement whatever. The river is beautiful here, of course, but a little dull . . . On the right you can follow, if you look close, the almost submerged remains of the old Muscle Shoals Canal . . . How narrow that canal was, how very conservatively it hugged that low bluff on the north bank! How narrow, how conservative in comparison with this radical ocean-stretch of lake water before us, smooth and featureless!

At his journey's end there is this entry:

June 9, 1942. Coming into Paducah at early daylight . . .
It is time to go.
Farewell, Paducah. Farewell to the Tennessee . . .

Farewell, for a long, long time to the Indian river, to the river of the pioneers, to the steamboats and gunboats and mussel boats. New times, new customs have made you look new, but you are very old. What dove will fly over your deluge, bringing word of still newer change, we cannot know.

☆ | 7 | ☆

'LECTRIC LIGHTS

"When the moon shines over the cowshed there will be a light inside." A banner bearing these words was jauntily displayed by children from a small country school as they marched down the streets of Tupelo, Mississippi, on November 3, 1933. Tupelo was the first municipality to receive the new electric power from the reservoirs and powerhouses on the Tennessee River. TVA's directors had just arrived to sign the contract. Director Arthur Morgan described their reception:

I was wholly unaware of any plans for a public ceremony, and was surprised to find the entire district turned out for the occasion. Especially the farmers of the county and their families were in evidence.

There was a parade of children from the rural school districts which illustrated how to these people the coming of electricity means a new day.

Not only for Tupelo. By late 1933, farmers of a dozen counties in Mississippi and Alabama were already constructing rural transmission lines to tap the electricity from the Tennessee River.

They did so mainly because TVA offered low rates, far

lower than those of Commonwealth and Southern, the private power utility that had, before TVA, dominated the valley. But the TVA directors hoped that cheap electricity would encourage a greater demand for it. People who had not imagined they could afford a light bill would be able to pay it now. And, with greater overall consumer use of electricity, TVA could afford to keep rates down.

So people began signing up. People like this Tennessean, recorded by a Works Progress Administration researcher, who well recalled how it had been "before":

Pa an' some of my older brothers carried hand lights. These lights wuz made of light'ood pine splinters. 'Bout six or eight of the splinters wuz bundled together an' lit at the end. They give a good light. Sometimes I got me some splinters an' carried me a hand light, too. The splinters wuz put out when the house wuz reached an' if they hadn't burnt up 'till they wuz too short they wuz lit and used on the return trip home after prayer meetin' wuz over. Most everybody carried fresh splinters along for hand lights in case the ones lit wuz burnt up 'fore the house visited wuz reached.

But now every day marked the coming of electricity to homes in the valley. Local newspapers told of the impact of the light bulb on twentieth-century families. Sometimes the flick of the switch was like a holiday—the fireworks Tennesseans set off at Christmas. Here is a story from the Chattanooga, Tennessee, *Times:*

*Farm children doing their homework
by kerosene lamps.*

Far up the side of Nubbin Ridge in the Cumberlands the small, neat home of Grandpaw and Grandmaw Forbus was the scene of feverish activity on Christmas Eve day of a recent year.

Grandmaw had been gone over a week ministering to a daughter in the valley whose third child was now a week old. During her absence Grandpaw and his two sons at home had been preparing a big Christmas surprise . . .

The lamps were lit and Grandpaw and the boys were sitting by the fire when the chugging of a car of ancient vintage toiling up the ridge road informed them that Blanche's husband was bringing Grandmaw home.

"Blow out them lamps!" Grandpaw ordered. They stepped to the door and waited in the darkness as Grandmaw climbed from the car and started up the path. The old man stepped back into the room as his weary wife reached the door and in the darkness he groped for the new fixture which would provide the family's Christmas present.

"Surprise! Surprise!" he called as he pulled a chain and flooded the room with what seemed blinding light. "Merry Christmas, Maw!" the two boys yelled. Mrs. Forbus rubbed her eyes, at first because of the brightness and then in an effort to brush away her tears of happiness. Grandpaw Forbus was scurrying from room to room, pulling chains, turning the new electric lights on and off.

Finally he got back to the sitting room, where Grandmaw still stood. He gave the cord a couple of pulls, turning the light off and back on again. He was laughing and crying both. He looked at his wife; she was crying. "Ain't it wonderful?" he blubbered. "'Lectric lights after all these years!"

Over the air began to come the voices of Fred Allen and Jimmy Durante and the fortunes of "Fibber McGee and Molly" and "The Great Gildersleeve." Radio connected the back-country farmers, in a sense, with the mainstream of American life. They guffawed along with everybody else at Jack Benny.

DON: Ladies and gentlemen, it has been said that Jack Benny has brought more laughs to more people than any man who ever lived. And now I bring you the man who said it—Jack Benny! (Applause.)

MARY: Don—Don, you wasted that introduction because Jack isn't here yet.

DON: He isn't? Where is he?

PHIL: Maybe he followed some babe down Vine Street and forgot to look up when he passed N.B.C.

DON: Don't be silly, Phil. Jack doesn't follow girls.

MARY: He doesn't, eh? How do you think he met me? . . .

JACK: [Entering]: . . . Do you know what's happened to me?

PHIL: We know, we know.

DON: Yes, Jack, Mary told us that Warner Brothers were going to make a picture about your life.

JACK: Yes, sir, the same studio that made the life of Emile Zola, the life of Louis Pasteur, the life of

Mark Twain. And now, the life of Jack Benny.
(Fanfare of two trumpets.)

JACK: Now cut that out. Smart-aleck musicians . . .

PHIL: All right, so what's interesting about your life?

JACK: Mine is a story of adventure and courage. The
real true life of Jack Benny. (Fanfare of two
trumpets.)

JACK: Now stop with that. Enough's enough. Listen,
Phil, you may not believe this, but my life has
been one adventure after another. It started
when I ran away from home to face the world all
by myself.

PHIL: How old were you?

MARY: Thirty-two.

JACK: I was twenty-seven. I remember because I didn't
want to leave until I finished high school. Thirty-
two. And look what happened to me after that.
Broadway, vaudeville, musical comedy, radio!
Why, when they make the picture of my life it'll
be as long as Gone with the Wind.

MARY: It should be, they both started in the same
period.

The coming of electricity provided back-country
farmers not only parlor light and the humor of Jack
Benny in the sitting room, but also less back-breaking
ways of living and farming. One reporter overheard this:
"I suppose you will buy a curling iron now?" one Tupelo
woman was asked just before the cheap power was turned
on. "No," she said. "The first thing I buy will be an
electric pump to put water into my kitchen sink."

Or it might be a butter churn. The Knoxville *News Sentinel* quoted Mr. and Mrs. S. J. Cox, on Texas Valley Road: "I sure was glad to hear we could get electricity at TVA rates," Mr. Cox said, "And I told the man it would be worth the whole $6 a month I promised to use in power to get the juice wired to my butter churn." The electric-driven churn was the apple of Mr. Cox's eye:

"It used to take both my boy and me to turn it," he said. "Now, if you've ever been on the crank of a butter churn with 30 or 40 gallons of milk in it, for an hour, you can appreciate this," and he pointed to the motor hitched by a belt to a wooden wheel on the side of the churn.

"Just pull the switch—that's all you have to do," he said gleefully.

Mrs. Cox was just as exuberant.

"Look at my new electric stove," she said, "Just think, no ashes for my husband to carry out, no wood to chop or anything."

In the early days, director David Lilienthal himself sometimes acted as a salesman of electrical appliances. Writing in his *Journal: The TVA Years,* he describes his experience in salesmanship:

I used to make speeches before country crowds with a lot of farm machinery gadgets (grinders for feed, brooders, etc.) set up on a big table in front of me and would work these into the talk, indicating how much some particular farmer somewhere had added to his net income when he had these machines (most of which we designed ourselves, to meet the problems of these poor farmers, poor compared to the farmers of the North for whom the big manufacturers had previously done all their work).

Though Mr. Lilienthal felt his method to be undignified—"like an Indian root doctor"—he knew that his audience listened to every word.

In the office of the REA [Rural Electrification Administration] in town, on the rather dingy courthouse square . . . there were a few electric appliances. Farm women, very nice-looking indeed, were looking at the shining white porcelain with evident enjoyment. It is not a new sight to me, but it always quickens me a bit. The electric water pump demonstration had one farmer entranced; kept turning the faucet on and off, fascinated. This is something that isn't just oratory; they can understand it . . .

They came up afterwards and handled the gadgets and watched the electric motor grind feed, etc. And then a co-op would be formed and the power lines would reach them; but they got more than power; they got a lift to their dragging morale, they got a bit of economic education, the only way they could, by a demonstration . . .

Rural electric cooperatives were being formed throughout the valley. At one, in Dalton, Georgia, a TVA director explained how electric power compared with the muscle power of the farmer and his work team.

I have never understood why the electric industry invented the term "kilowatt." I wish they had stuck to a simple word like horsepower. Horsepower is a word you and I can understand. When we say a tractor has 50 horsepower, we know just what it means; we know that it has a pulling power or a working power that is roughly equal to the strength of 50 horses.

The word kilowatt, of course, means working power also, but the word itself does not convey the same down-to-earth meaning. It sounds technical, and it is. Recently I tried to figure out some way to make this word kilowatt make sense. This is what I came up with and I thought it might interest you.

The mechanical engineers, I find, have given a very precise definition to the term horsepower. All horses, naturally, do not have the same working power, but for the mechanical engineers they do. One horsepower is the energy or force required to lift a weight of 550 pounds a distance of one foot in one second. A man, they estimate—and we'll say an average man—can do about one-tenth the work of a horse . . .

Now the electrical engineers come on the scene. They have a way of translating the work energy of one horsepower to kilowatts, or electrical power. One horsepower, they say, equals about 750 watts. The energy of a man, then, would be one-tenth of that, or about 75 watts.

Now suppose that a man works eight hours a day, five days a week, for fifty weeks during a year. On that basis in a year's time he puts in about 2,000 hours of work. Multiply this 2,000 by 75 watts and you find that this man has put out working energy equal to 150,000 watt hours, or (since 1,000 watts equals 1 kilowatt) 150 kilo-watt-hours (kwh) in a year.

That was the backache value of electricity. What about the dollar-and-cents value? The new electricity was the "biggest bargain in the history of the world," continued the director.

Now let's take our figuring a step further. The average residential rate for electricity in the Tennessee Valley area is a little over one cent per kilowatt-hour, 1.03 cents to be exact. Multiply 150 kilowatt-hours by 1.03 cents and you get a result which to me is quite phenomenal. The electric equivalent of the work of a man for an entire year costs one dollar and fifty-five cents!

Is this amazing to you? It is to me. Yet it is true.

With the farmer's heaviest physical burdens lifted, farm families were spurred to improve their living conditions in general. Capping an article appearing in 1940 in the Knoxville *News Sentinel* was this headline: "HOW CHEAP ELECTRICITY PEPS UP A FARM: TRANSFORMATION OF MISSISSIPPI PLACE." First the article pictured the farm before electricity came:

It then had no running water, no paint on the house, a wood range, and the kitchen was clean but dark.

The only kitchen window then opened out on a low wide back porch. On the farm, cotton then was the main crop. Scarcely enough feed stuff was raised for home use . . .

The first year he [the farmer] put in a pump, washing machine and refrigerator. The washing machine and pump released time and energy for other things . . . The returns from his refrigerator average $30 a month. This income is received from butter and milk.

As the years went on, he increased his electrical equipment by adding an incubator, brooder, motor, churn, lights in laying house yard, and laundry.

A comparison of *before* and *after* worked out in dollars and cents showed:

In 1936 he had 50 hens, one cow and two pigs . . . For 1940, his plans include 300 hens, four cows, five pigs and two head of beef cattle.

The net income from his farm, including family living, in 1936 was $700 . . . In 1939 it was $1,700.

The very idea of progress seemed to stimulate other improvements:

In 1939 a bath was added to the six-room house. Only weeds were around the house at the start of the development, but now there is an attractive lawn, planted with native shrubs, and the house is painted white . . .

The kitchen remodeled now has built-in cabinets, hot and cold running water, painted walls, linoleum on floors, and a nice pantry. It is equipped with an electric mixer, toaster, churn and hotplate . . .

In a much larger sense, electricity seemed to offer a way out of the nationwide farm problem. Dating from the mid-1920s into the 1930s, there had been surpluses. The nation's farmers as a whole were producing more than consumers would buy. During the depression, when

"And there was light"—
a farmyard scene in
Lincoln County, Tennessee.

money was scarce, farm produce flooded the market. Prices dropped disastrously.

An article in the Indianapolis, Indiana, *Times*, April 17, 1935, suggested at least a partial solution for the Tennesse valley. It involved electricity:

Today, a farmer is absolutely dependent upon his market. Most of the things he raises are perishable and he has no way to store them for a good price. If he has 10 dozen eggs on hand, he has to get rid of them, whether eggs are bringing 5 cents a dozen or 20 cents a dozen. He cannot even save them for his own use . . .

He may sell a hog to the local butcher for 4 cents a pound and then buy it back over a period of time in the form of dressed meat at 12 to 14 cents a pound. [To try to pay for the meat, he raises more hogs.] When there is a surplus of farm products, he still has to keep increasing that surplus and further flooding of the market.

The only method discovered thus far for preventing this disastrous surplus is the expensive one of paying the farmer with government money to plow under cotton and to slaughter his livestock.

TVA has another plan not involving this enormous expense and waste. It is based upon cheap electricity. A group of farmers in a county would get together in a voluntary co-operative. Each one puts a few dollars into a fund. A storage and refrigeration plant is built.

When the price of hogs is too low, the farmer simply takes his pigs to the general co-operative warehouse and stores them in an electrically refrigerated atmosphere. There the meat will hang, available for sale or handy for him and his neighbors to use on their own tables.

Such a plan would make the farmer self-sustaining and prevent the awful surpluses of the past few years.

At the end of the article, the *Times* added this: "Private utility interests have kicked up such a cloud of dust around the TVA and its power policies that the issue is not clear in the minds of many people."

Yes, it seemed as if nothing could be done in the Tennessee valley without a fight. It was not surprising that the cheap electricity was fought all the way by the private utilities, who feared the loss of their market. But many "little people" were fearful, too. United Press reported a hot-tempered reaction from Milwaukee in February 27, 1933:

SEES TVA START GIGANTIC HAND TO COST MANY JOBS

Milwaukee, Feb. 27. The Tennessee Valley power project was compared to the "Butcher's hand on the scales cheating the customer" by Stephen Bolles, editor of the Janesville Gazette in an address here.

An extended trip through the Tennessee Valley convinced him, Bolles said, that the chief object of the project was the creation of a gigantic power kingdom which will destroy private companies in the Valley and throw 2,000,000 persons out of work.

"The TVA will cost taxpayers $2,000,000,000," he said. "It is the wolf in sheep's clothing; the beautiful sepulcher filled with dead men's bones."

But just how well had private utilities worked for the valley in the past? Commonwealth and Southern, like

In 1933, a cartoonist for the
Chicago Tribune predicted that TVA's
cheap electricity would benefit big corporations,
such as the aluminum trust, rather
than the people of the valley.

most of the nation's private utilities, had waited for increased use by consumers to justify lowering their rates. When TVA first came, fewer than 3 percent of the farms were supplied with electric current. The picture in one state—Alabama—was reported by *Harper's* magazine in January 1939:

Until recently the Southern units of the Commonwealth and Southern had been cultivating only the most prosperous strata in their area . . . In all the homes of rural Alabama served by the company in December, 1932, there were run on electricity only 645 iceboxes, 85 sewing machines, 185 vacuum cleaners, 700 radios. In all the thousands of square miles controlled by the Alabama Power Company the use of electric power in rural homes and farms was equivalent, the year before TVA, to no more than can be found in a good city block.

Even under the supposedly watchful eyes of public commissioners, which most states had in the 1930s, the system of private power ownership had not been working too well. If it had been, the TVA power question would not immediately have become such a burning issue.

Commonwealth and Southern carried its fight to the Supreme Court. Its chief public spokesman was Wendell Willkie, later to become a presidential candidate.

As the issue was being debated in court, the same *Harper's* article showed, much of the nation could not decide who was right in the private versus federal utilities fight.

At about the time when these words appear in print —perhaps even before they appear—the most litigated battle in the most litigated industry in the world will have reached its climax. The United States Supreme Court will have handed down a decision in the case of the Commonwealth and Southern Corporation versus the Tennessee Valley Authority. The time seems appropriate to analyze the many-sided problem thus brought to issue; for the case offers, in microcosm, an incomparable economic and social history of the modern corporation in its relation to the American public.

In New York City sits the registrar of a great university. Occasionally through the day his mind wanders from aptitude tests and freshmen to the 20 shares of preferred stock which he owns in Commonwealth and Southern. He paid $100 apiece for them nine years ago, and now they are down to about $50. He wonders about the TVA and his investment.

Down by Bear Creek, between Tuscumbia and Tupelo, in the corn and cotton belt of the South, Cliff Jenkins these days often comes in from the fields and meditates upon his fortunes. Eight years ago he had 40 acres of eroded gullies and hard lands—and little hope. Today . . . by virtue of having electric lights and operating an electric brooder and using a number of other economically useful electric devices, he is known as an "electro-development farmer." Cliff Jenkins wonders about his investment in TVA.

Between these two very real men stand Main Street and Wall Street. Opinion in Wall Street is reasonably united: it holds that a government intent on socialistic

The Memphis Press-Scimitar's
cartoonist was all for TVA.

adventure and on the harassing of privately-owned utilities has gone into destructive competition with these utilities; and that, if not checked by the high court, it will embark on new power projects and in effect ruin investment values in the utilities wherever it may choose to compete with them.

TVA's investment in power potential had been considerable. In 1935 director Arthur Morgan estimated that the total cost of Wheeler Dam, for example, would be about $29,500,000. Some 30 percent was charged off to navigation; the rest—$19,760,000—to the dam's power potential. So now the TVA directors argued their point of view with real concern. In one instance, Morgan spoke out:

Those who buy electric current in our cities seldom have any choice as to whom they buy it from. There usually is but one source. They must pay the standard price or go without . . . for these various reasons it is evident that the business of supplying electricity is a public business, and that those who carry on that business are under moral obligation to carry it on primarily as a public service . . .

President Franklin Roosevelt was another who was deeply and vigorously in favor of public power if the private utilities failed to satisfy their customers. In a speech delivered in Portland, Oregon, in 1933, he had said:

I lay down the following principle: That where a community, a city, or county, or a district is not satisfied with the service rendered or the rates charged by the private utility, it has the undeniable right as one of its functions of government, as one of the functions of home rule, to set up, after a fair referendum has been taken, its own governmentally owned and operated service . . .

The very fact that a community can, by vote of the electorate, create a yardstick of its own, will, in most cases, guarantee good service and low rates to its population. I might call the right of the people to own and operate their own utility a "birch rod in the cupboard, to be taken out and used only when the child gets beyond the point where scolding does any good."

In late 1939 the Supreme Court made its decision: it ruled that TVA power *was* constitutional.

As it turned out, TVA was not the "wolf in sheep's clothing" the Milwaukee editor had feared. The Indianapolis *Times* reported that "Subscribers in Tupelo, which has a population of 6361, saved a little more than $100,000 a year in rates. In Athens, where live 4236 people, savings to electrical customers were $30,000 a year." Even the private utilities of the region fared better after the coming of cheap electricity. Over twenty years, private utilities expanded 150 percent on the nationwide average. But in the eight states adjacent to Tennessee, power capacity owned by private utilities increased 200 percent.

Today a network of rural lines throughout the countryside brings electricity within the reach of almost every farmsite, no matter how remote from the city. Some 6 million people in an area of 80,000 square miles are served.

Nevertheless, despite all, TVA's public power policy remains controversial. Until 1959, when it issued public bonds, its funds had to be provided annually by Congress, and sometimes TVA was starved for operating money. At other times it has been threatened with sale. It has been called "creeping socialism" by no less a person than President Dwight D. Eisenhower.

One Watertown, Tennessee, woman had a hot retort to the President. She wrote a letter to the *Nashville Tennessean*, published August 6, 1953:

To the Editor:

For 50 years I have been a resident of Tennessee. For 40 years I have been a farmer's wife, living in the so-called "good old days." We had kerosene lamps, the old fashioned kind, then the wonderful Aladdin, then came TVA, more wonderful to me than anything I ever had—even the Model-A Ford. I had rather pay the light bill than any other . . .

Perhaps if a few lights at our nation's capital were cut out Dwight would consider them more beneficial and reconsider our country homes needing the cheap power we are now getting . . .

Mrs. Pauline Oakley

☆ | 8 | ☆

GRASS ROOTS

Just take the Tennessee Valley [wrote James Agee in Fortune magazine in 1935]. By quality and by geography, it breaks very roughly into three parts. By quality it is a third good, a third middling, a third godawful, nearly all in danger. Geographically; the east and north are steep, planted much to corn when planted at all, sickly most of it, rooked with gullies. The west and south are gentler sloping, wearied with a surfeit of cotton, slowly more sterile year by year, year by year quite surely sloughing its skin. In three or four of the middle counties there is land as rich as any on this continent, and the wounds of rain heal swiftly level as the harmed flesh of a healthy child, for this land overlies phosphate beds. But elsewhere in the valley you would hardly set a camera down and fail to get some record of the great mange of the land.

The "mange of the land" had meant poor corn, cotton, and tobacco crops and low prices all through the 1920s and 1930s. At the time, a blues writer, Sampson Pittman, echoed the farmer's familiar lament about "Seven Cent Cotton and Forty Cent Meat" in a popular song of that name. He wrote, "These blues was composed in nineteen and twenty seven on the condition of the farmers and on the shortness of their cotton. I thought it was very necessary to put out a record of these things. I composed them of the necessity of the farmers. It was very popular among everyone that heard it . . ."

Seven Cent Cotton and Forty Cent Meat

Sev - en cent cot - ton and for - ty cent meat,

How in the world can a poor man eat?

Flo - ur up high and cot - ton down low,

How in the world can we raise the dough?

Clothes worn out, shoes run down, Old slouch hat with a

hole in the crown: Back near - ly brok - en and

fin - gers all sore, Cot - ton gone down to rise no more.

Seven cent cotton and forty cent meat,
How in the world can a poor man eat?
Mules in the barn, no crops laid by,
Corn crib empty and the cow's gone dry.
Well water low, nearly out of sight,
Can't take a bath on Saturday night.
No use talking, any man is beat
With seven cent cotton and forty cent meat.

Seven cent cotton and eight dollar pants,
Who in the world has got a chance?
We can't buy clothes and we can't buy meat,
Too much cotton and not enough to eat.
Can't help each other, what shall we do?
I can't explain it so it's up to you.
Seven cent cotton and two dollar hose,
Guess we'll have to do without any clothes.

Seven cent cotton and forty cent meat
How in the world can a poor man eat?
Poor getting poorer all around here,
Kids coming regular every year.
Fatten our hogs, take 'em to town,
All we get is six cents a pound.
Very next day we have to buy it back,
Forty cents a pound in a paper sack.

By 1935 TVA power lines were humming over some pastures and hillsides, and great concrete dams were rising to intercept the course of the Tennessee. But even with flood control, a smooth-flowing river, and cheap electricity, how could the largely rural population rise out of despondency unless some attention were paid to the land?

Luckily, during the 1930s the national attitude toward natural resources was more enlightened than it had been in the earlier days of Gifford Pinchot and George Norris. The conservation idea was beginning to catch fire. By 1935 a local Georgia man was writing concernedly in the *Towns County Herald:*

What will the future generations do with these old gullies and how are they going to make a living on them?

What would you say of a man who rented your horse and starved him in such a way that he would be useless to you afterwards? . . .

Or what would you think of a man who would drive your car in such a manner as to strip the gears, destroy the casing and batter up the body? You would not like it and would say so.

The rising generations who are going to have to try to get a living out of these Georgia farms are going to say something about those who have had the management of the farms in Georgia for the last generation . . .

It was opinion from the grass roots. On the national level, President Roosevelt had equally strong views, particularly regarding forests. The idea of TVA had included from the first a massive land-reclamation program, and now it began—under Roosevelt's auspices—with forestry. A network of tree roots could hold the soil back in time of flooding and prevent gullies and erosion. A tree crop, planted on hillsides where corn and cotton should never have been grown, could also help restore minerals to the soil. As director David Lilienthal said, "Saving the soil is the first step—to keep the soil from washing away;

to save its fertility from being hopelessly exhausted. For the soil is the nation's basic resource."

TVA's forestry division consisted of about fifty men. They were to advise landowners how to administer and develop the valley's timberlands—some 14 million acres, or more than 54 percent of the valley land. Through reforestation—planting new seedlings on former farmlands and replanting burned-over timberlands—they hoped to stop erosion at its very roots. As tree crops could also be profitable, nurseries were developed, a living laboratory for the study of the best timber possibilities for the Tennessee valley.

Fifty men, of course, did not do all the digging and spading. In the same *Fortune* article, James Agee called the forestry division but the "architects" of the job. "The 'contractors' and the laborers," he wrote, "are the twenty CCC camps, the 6,000 CCC boys who are doing the most pressing and immediately necessary chapter of the work."

The CCC boys—members of the Civilian Conservation Corps, one of Roosevelt's first New Deal agencies—formed a veritable army by 1935. There were 600,000 of them, more than five times the size of the regular army at the time.

Many of the workers in the CCC came to realize that what they were doing had far more significance than just getting a job. Said one young man interviewed by a WPA researcher:

As I say, I don't know just when it happened, but all at once I became conscious of the glorious opportunity before me. Why, here was not only a chance to help support my family, but to do something bigger—to help on to success this part of the President's daring new plan to down Old Man Depression.

Patriotism groaned in my soul, turned, and woke up. Bits of "My Country 'Tis of Thee" floated in my mind. Yes, sir!

From the same *Fortune* article comes this picture of what the CCC boys did in the valley, with spades and shovels and seedlings.

Work is concentrated just now within the 1,856,000 acres that comprise the entire watershed about Norris Dam: fifteen of the CCC camps are in that region. They attacked first the lower half-million acres where erosion is most active and most critical, will soon climb toward and into Virginia. They use these four types of check dam: burlap bags part filled with soil and sprinkled with grass seed are laid in the washes and the shallow troughs. Brush dams stop gullies too deep for bags. Deeper gullies take log-and-plank dams up to five feet high. And, toward the lower end of big-time gullies, or wherever the drainage will be permanent, rock and mortar dams are built up to eight feet high. Besides which, all steep and galled land is staked and wired over with brush matting sown with grass seed. Best week's work for one camp: over 200 rock dams: better than one a week per man. CCC accomplishment up to January 1, 1935:

> 27,826 rock dams
> 28,331 log dams

```
    2,866  brush dams
   23,578  bag dams
5,446,491  yards of brush matting
    6,000  acres of timber-stand improvement
   45,000  yards of diversion ditches
      200  miles of truck trails
      130  vehicle bridges
```

But, added Agee, "All that is mere preliminaries":

Check dams and brush matting slow the runoff and baste down the soil until a cover of grass or vines or shrubs or, most permanently of all, trees, weft it forever into place. They are trying every kind of cover—Bermuda grass behind the dams, bush clover (lespedeza) where sheet erosion is most virulent, even honeysuckle, which every Tennessean despises: it will grow not merely all over your land but in your ears at the slightest encouragement. And, by the millions, trees: not merely the famously efficient black locust (5,000,000 of these) but trees of much greater timber value—the black walnut, the tulip poplar, a whole assortment of oaks and pines, the blight-resistant Asiatic chestnut.

Cooperating with the CCC boys were tens of thousands of farmers, each working on his own land. In the old days farmers had been in the habit of saying:

> A *sloping field,*
> A *surface bare,*
> A *heavy rain—*
> And *the soil ain't there.*

Now they were saying:

> A *sloping field,*
> A *clover cover—*
> *The water soaks in*
> *Somehow or other.*

Forest agencies contributed with a search for superior trees—trees with above-average genetic characteristics in terms of size, wood quality, disease resistance. Twigs from these trees were grafted to the root systems of ordinary seedlings of the same species, and the grafted plants were then set out in orchards. In this way, superior seeds for new plantings were developed, with superior forests in view as the end product.

Now, with dams on the gullied land as well as on the river, with sprouting ground cover and firmly rooted trees holding the soil in place, what about the crops for which the land was hopefully being readied?

TVA's agricultural program began at the grass roots, with the farmer himself. Agricultural agents from the land-grant colleges talked to farmers face to face on their own fields. Slowly and often skeptically an enterprising few learned: To divert some of their worn-out corn or cotton fields to grazing lands for livestock. To terrace and contour-plow their sloping land to keep gullies from forming. To use fertilizer so that new sod could successfully cover the bleeding earth.

TVA had already been authorized by Congress to manufacture and sell "fertilizer and fertilizer ingredients," using the existing facilities for nitrate production at Muscle Shoals. Yes, during all this time, the

---

"The famously efficient black locust":
left to right, cluster of flowers, winter twig,
details of leaf scar and imbedded buds (enlarged),
branch with mature leaves, and fruits.

obsolete World War I plant for making ammonium nitrate—which could be turned into either fertilizer or munitions—had been kept in standby condition under the National Defense Act. Now, after thoroughgoing research and experimentation, electric furnaces, using the new Tennessee River power, were built to convert the rock phosphate of middle Tennessee to elementary phosphorus. Then, through a series of chemical treatments, the phosphorus was finally converted to *concentrated superphosphate*. Most superphosphate ran about 16 to 20 percent plant food (P_2O_5); TVA's *concentrated* was about 45 percent.

But creating a more potent plant food was not enough. It had to be used, and few indeed were the farmers willing to try it. In his *Journal*, David Lilienthal tells an anecdote about how one farmer was convinced. Lilienthal picked up the story from an "old boy" at a community soil meeting in Mississippi in 1941:

When it rained, the farmer sat in his cabin and listened to the rain on his cotton field and knew for sure that it was spoiling his cotton. On top of that, he always had to worry about whether or not he would get anything for his cotton when the season was over. He had a cow and her name was Bessie. He didn't like cows, and especially didn't like Bessie. In fact, he hated Bessie. Every day Bessie would wander away and he would have to go out and look for her. Most likely she was in the cornfield of some neighbor down the road. The neighbor would raise hell, and the farmer would have to beat Bessie and drag her back home.

This happened nearly every day until he could hardly stand the sight of Bessie. But then came TVA phosphate. He put it on his land, and lo and behold, the clover began to grow and it wasn't long before he staked Bessie out in the clover and grass. After that, Bessie stayed at home because this kind of feeding was just her meat. She stayed at home, eating the luscious TVA-phosphated grass and didn't go wandering off into his neighbor's cornfield. Pretty soon he began to see that Bessie had some good points. In fact, he became right fond of Bessie, and so he covered some more of his cotton land with phosphate and lime, and now he has eleven cows, "by God," and now he likes cows, and he calls every one of them Bessie on account of now he likes Bessie so much.

Most farmers, struggling with their unyielding acres, had first to be convinced in hard dollar-and-cents terms of the worth of the new fertilizer to them. The plan adopted was imaginative—creating thousands of test demonstrations throughout the valley. Volunteer farmers, chosen by their neighbors, carried out live demonstrations of modern farming with the new phosphate fertilizer, coupled with up-to-date machinery and electricity. At their own risk, these farmers broke with tradition to undertake a changed way of farming and of life.

One such farmer was Robert Hannabas. When TVA came to the valley he had a ninety-three-acre farm purchased in 1917. The land was in Washington County, Tennessee. Hannabas spoke of the test demonstration farm idea as "an unfolding one, just like turning the leaves of a book or seeing an interesting story developed in the movies."

I remember very distinctly the first chapter in my demonstration program. My steep 93-acre farm is all bottom land. The top had washed away before I got it.

I really started the test program when I drilled phosphate on clover on one of my steep hills and drove down some stakes to mark off the check plot. The results were far beyond my expectations . . . It was soon learned that these stakes were not necessary, as the green strips showed plainly . . . after one field, we began to see results on all the fields, on lespedeza, clover, pasture and other soil protecting crops.

Hannabas went on to describe the value of all this new greenery:

I was producing great yields and more legumes [a source of nitrogen for the soil]. I could keep more livestock. I needed to make changes in my system of farming . . . The Agricultural Extension Service advised me to cultivate less row crops and grow more alfalfa and have more and better permanent pasture . . . A new day was started on my old farm . . .

It was along about this time that my friends began to tell me that they had heard the same thing would happen to me back in 1918, 1919 and 1920 that had happened to three or four owners of this farm prior to me, namely, "starve out." (Sometimes I had thought I would.)

But the fact that Robert Hannabas was no longer in the slightest danger of "starving out" attracted the curiosity and attention of his friends.

My neighbors began to notice that something was happening to my farm and to me. Things were different. They visited my place individually and in groups, and they too wanted help. Working together we set up a community demonstration, and if I do say so myself, our people have really gone to town with their community demonstration program. Not only with the use of lime and phosphate but on many things that affect the farm and farm home.

Ten years after the establishment of TVA 20,000 farm families up and down the valley were test demonstrators. Their efforts were a three-way partnership between the farmer himself, the extension service of the land-grant colleges, and TVA, the supplier of fertilizers.

The efforts were fruitful. In 1943 David Lilienthal wrote:

If you fly over the region today you look down upon a land that has experienced a marked and unmistakable change. Fields that were washing away are covered with sod; gullies that were raw are healing with checkdams and locust; millions of trees have been set out on badly eroded slopes; almost everywhere you see from the air the graceful designs drawn by terracing and contour plowing. Millions of acres are being restored, and more than acres—hope, too, is being restored.

Some of the people in the valley remained unimpressed. They questioned the value of "progress." Why all the scrambling for the dollar and modern life's swifter

*The plow has followed the contours
of the land on this demonstration farm
in Madison County, North Carolina.*

pace? In her book *Kith and Kin in Tennessee,* author Elmora Messer Matthews recounted gossip to this effect that she heard swapped in the ridges of Tennessee:

That feller is never satisfied—always pushin'. If he had three acres of tobacco to cut, he'd want it cut in one day.

He's too ole to work, but he works anyway. That man would do anything fur a dollar.

I never owned a car or tractor. I farmed from the time I was six years old, and I made fifty-six tobacco crops. I got all my livin' out of fifty acres, dug it out of the dirt. I raised twelve kids, but every one of 'em got crossed up, tryin' to make money.

Some folks is too smart.

What most of us needs is some common sense. A man's got to come to his right knowin'.

Modern life or no, a *better* life for all the people of the valley was still a long way off and TVA knew it well. The fate of the sharecropper was still an unsolved problem. In 1935 there were some 19,000 black farm operators, and over 12,000 of them were tenants or sharecroppers. The TVA farm program was of little use to them.

When TVA first bought up land to flood, the purchase was usually with the white landowner. Black croppers and tenants, who were merely renting, simply lost their homes. A side effect of the agricultural program, too, was to push blacks off the land. As crops were diversified away from cotton and corn and as farms became more and more mechanized, the farmhands and pickers had to turn elsewhere for work. Many moved into developing industries brought to the region by cheap electricity. Others migrated out of the South altogether. Between 1930 and 1950, the rural Negro population of the valley dropped 15 percent.

Richard Wright eloquently described the feeling of being dispossessed in a story called "Fire and Cloud." A black congregation was praying:

"The white folks say we can't raise nothin' on yo earth! They done put the lans of the worl' in their pockets. They done fenced 'em off n' nailed 'em down! Theys a-tryin' t' take yo place, Lawd!"

A bulletin prepared by the Tuskegee Institute in 1953, called *Negro Farmers in the Tennessee Valley*, described the changing scene. On one plantation

an old man, who had lived there all of his life, was sitting on a porch watching a tractor rumble across the field. He complained about being idle while the tractor plowed. He insisted he was perfectly able to plow his own crop with mules. He did not realize, or at least did not admit, that he remained there practically a pensioner of a landlord who was sentimental about his years of past labor.

On a plantation where tractors were just being intro-duced, a landlord had nailed up recently emptied cabins. Cows grazing around a stark old chimney which stood in a pasture seemed poetic symbolism. This was only one of many vacant spots where houses once stood.

A young sharecropper harvesting tobacco.

It was the beginning of the end for the established order of row-crop cultivation by the share-tenant system. An old way of life was disappearing.

To the 1 percent of farm-owners in the valley who were black, however, TVA fertilizer was sold as to others. The number of Negro demonstration farmers was roughly the ratio between white and nonwhite full-owner operators in the valley.

Getting out from under the tyranny of King Cotton meant change must come. The Cotton South had never been good to blacks, and some of the change was bound to be positive. The Tuskegee bulletin commented:

In one place there is an old chimney in a new pasture. In another place there is a new comfortable house in place of the old cabin. In one place there are tractors equipped with umbrellas to shade drivers moving through growing cotton plants with no row of cabins along the way to prevent watching them tirelessly plow and plow more. . . . Only a part of the family income comes from cotton. Regular wages earned by members of the family from employment in industries make a difference.

Industries did indeed make a difference, and many were coming to the Tennessee valley. Cheap power was attracting enterprises that involved the electrochemical or electrometallurgical treatment of native rocks and minerals—processes requiring large amounts of electricity. Others came to develop the reviving resources of the region, to process and can farm produce, to manufacture pulp and paper products from the forests and woodlots. The world's largest newsprint mill, for example, came to locate in a southeastern Tennessee corn-field.

In forestry, as in farming, the technique of test demonstrations was employed. One experiment went on at the Hassell and Hughes Lumber Company in the Highland Rim country of western Tennessee. The average woodland there was so depleted that the task of recovery seemed almost hopeless.

But Hassell and Hughes' officials, after reviewing the possibilities with TVA and state foresters, decided to invest and develop rather than sell out—even though they knew it would be a long, hard pull. R. M. Hughes, a partner in the firm, told the story of "The Road Back" in the March 1955 issue of the *Southern Lumberman*. "When in 1943," he said, "we acquired 49,000 acres of cut-over land . . . this was the turning point. We could see enough pine to keep us going for maybe five years. But we wanted to stay in business longer than that. Could we do it?" The advice the lumber company received was that the timberland could give lumber for more than five years, *if* there were some drastic changes made.

Our first big job was to get the fire situation under control . . . Today [ten years later] the average annual burn has been reduced from ten acres in every hundred to one in a hundred . . .

The next thing we had to do was find out how much and what kind of timber we had . . . On the basis of this information, we drew up a forest management plan to carry us through the next ten years.

A decade later, Hughes drew this conclusion:

We know our lands are in better shape. The average tree is larger in size, and the over-all quality of the timber is better . . . Fire is no longer a major problem . . . Our books show a satisfactory profit. We have found markets for the products we can best produce . . .

We're not worried about our future wood supply. We know exactly where it is coming from. We're growing it.

Other lumber companies learned from the example. TVA's forestry department reported that

This has been a true demonstration in the sense that it has convinced at least seventeen other landowners to initiate management on their 200,000 acres in the Highland Rim area.

And finally, foresters and forestry students beat a path to Hassell and Hughes' door to see and hear their success story at first hand.

At TVA's origin, Lilienthal had called its program of flood control, land recovery, power development, and human betterment a "seamless web." All the threads are hard to follow but certainly for many parts of the valley the phrase holds true. Many of the strands are interwoven in the story of one waterfront town, Decatur, Alabama. The economic depression of the 1930s had just about finished Decatur. The one major industry, a railroad shop that had employed 2,000 men, had closed. Several smaller industries had gone bankrupt. Seven of the eight banks in the county had closed.

In 1935 David Lilienthal had met with a small group

of public-minded Decatur citizens. Among them was the editor and publisher of Decatur's newspaper, Barrett Shelton. In Shelton's words, the group was "almost frankly hostile, for he represented to us another way of life. And our conversation might be summarized in this fashion. 'All right, you're here, you were not invited, but you're here. You are in command, now what are you going to do?' "

Reminiscing some years later, Barrett Shelton described what followed:

Dave leaned his chair back against the wall and the twinkle of a smile came into his eyes, as he said gently and firmly, "I'm not going to do anything. You're going to do it."

He went on to tell us something we never knew before. He went on to say that TVA would provide the tools of opportunity—flood control, malaria control, navigation on the river, low cost power, test-demonstration farming to show how our soils could be returned to fertility, a fertility lost through land erosion, another wayward child of a one-crop system. He told us the river would no longer defeat man, but would become the servant of man. "What you do with these tools," he said, "is up to you."

The group of Decatur citizens then and there decided that the old order, the old way of doing things had to change: "We could never again, if our people were to survive, allow ourselves to be dependent upon a one-industry and a one-crop system."

Our first step was to form our own Chamber of Commerce, formed at a time when most people didn't believe it could be done. There was very little money. So, with considerable struggle, we got together some cash and more pledges amounting to $3,000 for the budget the first year . . .

We then decided we were going to develop a cash market every day in the year for every farm product grown in the Decatur area. We were going to welcome industry, but not wait for it. We were going to develop our own farm processing plants.

We decided a packing plant would be the first venture and persuaded the local ice company to put in packing plant facilities when there wasn't as much as one wagon load of hogs in our whole county. We are now producing our own livestock to meet the demands of this market.

We then turned to milk, formed a little corporation with paid-in capital of $15,000, telling every stockholder to forget his investment, that he would never receive any return from his money anyway. What we were trying to do was establish a payroll every two weeks for the farm families of our section. The first day that plant went into operation there was a total supply of 1,800 pounds of milk. Today [1949], the production of milk pouring into this one plant peaks at 60,000 pounds and we have just started in this agricultural industry. What happened to the stockholders? Well, they never failed to receive six per cent annually on their money and about two months ago that little plant paid stockholders a 100 per cent dividend.

At about that time, navigation on the Tennessee had so improved that a Nebraskan flour firm located one of its new mills on Decatur's riverbank.

Here, you see, is an exciting example of what can happen when a liability is changed into an asset. The Tennessee wasn't navigable before the creation of TVA, there was no opportunity for a successful flour mill operation. Low-cost power didn't attract Nebraska Consolidated Mills Company to establish the Alabama Flour Mills at Decatur. Navigable water did it, plus the possibilities that flour could be produced at a cheaper cost per barrel owing to savings on freight. The impact of this industry on our section was tremendous. Farmers could grow grains because there was now a daily cash market. They could produce corn and wheat, and all the grains with assurance that they would sell their production. They could get cash for products for which previously there had been no market . . .

You can see by now that the opportunities which were at hand in the development of the river and the region were being seized upon by our people with renewed courage and confidence. We now knew that we couldn't be licked again, that what had been preached to us by TVA was economic truth.

Next, local industries started up, and

Today, there is a market for cotton, corn, wheat, livestock, milk, timber, small grains, truck crops. Fifteen years ago we were dozing in the sunshine waiting for that once-a-year payroll brought by cotton and wearing out our second finest resource, the land. Today the cash income from all farm products in the area surrounding Decatur is $43,000,000.

All these activities, land builders and man builders, said Barrett Shelton, could never have been pictured in the minds of a defeated people, of a people who the years before TVA came saw an uncontrolled river flood and wash away the best soil, erode the backlands, wash crops, houses, and barns down an angry stream. And what brought about the transformation in people's lives? "Land building did it. Flood control did it. Navigation did it. Malaria control did it. TVA, with the other State and Federal agricultural and health agencies, their teaching activated by an intelligent and determined people, did it.

"When visitors come into my section of the Valley," concluded the editor, "and ask, 'Wouldn't this all have happened without a TVA?' My answer to one and all is, 'It didn't!'"

☆ | 9 | ☆

ONE MAN'S HANDS

A single idea, deep in the convictions of men like Norris, Pinchot, the two Roosevelts, and others, had finally borne fruit. The idea that man and his environment are part of a "seamless web" had taken a long time to mature and a longer time still to find acceptance. Things had gone all the way down before the slow and painful upward climb began. Recall the near-death of the soil from continuous cotton and other row-crop plantings on steep hillsides; the brutal slaughter of the forests in the cut-out-and-get-out era; and—in an inevitable chain reaction—the floods washing everything before them; finally, the blight reaching out and touching the very people themselves.

Then a few "starry-eyed fanatics"—George Norris outstanding among them—began to wage a battle for these people, and indeed in behalf of all the people of the United States. He and his colleagues pitted themselves against those with vested interests and many others who shared their belief in unchecked private enterprise. The battle might well have been lost had not certain fateful events intervened. It took the menace of the Mississippi floods, in some part due to the tributaries of the Tennessee; it took the great depression, a disaster that brought into office Franklin D. Roosevelt—a "tree grower"—and his New Deal; it took all this to bring the dream to reality.

How well TVA succeeded in fulfilling the dream has been recorded in this book, often in the words of the people most directly concerned. We have glimpsed what it was like to have a river safe from flooding, smooth for travel, harnessed to light farmsteads, to ease the farmer's load and supply power for new industries that brought new jobs. We have seen what it meant to be able once again to have rich soil, healthy forests, sparkling waters. But most important, these transformations took place *with* people and not merely *for* them.

TVA was originally created not only to restore one great river valley, but also to contribute to the welfare of the nation as a whole. It was hoped that if the experiment were successful, every large river basin in the United States would have a similar valley authority. As a matter of fact, TVA did serve as a model for river planning in thirty-four foreign nations.

Over the course of the years, government officials, engineers, and students from all over the globe journeyed to America to see at first hand the Tennessee valley's great multipurpose project, and took home with them a wealth of exciting new ideas.

India's late Prime Minister Nehru, on a tour of the Tennessee valley in 1949, remarked, "The Authority has become legend in my country . . . a new type of institution . . . behind which lies a social purpose, a whole way of life." And India has embarked on three great multi-purpose river valley developments—the Damodar, the Mahandi, and the Sutley. The Chairman of the Damodar Valley Corporation said on a visit to TVA in 1958, "It is our model. We are copying it . . . We have sent many of our engineers over here to study it so we can avoid mistakes."

But in our own country the TVA experiment remains unique. The same profit-seeking private interests that had fought the idea from the beginning marshaled their forces to oppose each new attempt to create another TVA. Even more fundamental, David Lilienthal felt, was the attitude of certain federal bureaus centered in Washington—the Departments of Interior and Agriculture and the Army Corps of Engineers. These federal bureaus, he wrote, feared TVA's grass-roots approach and "its effective effort to decentralize the functioning of the federal government. . . . these fellows all see the danger to them of the TVA idea." And director Gordon Clapp added that "some of our country's leaders while applauding the idea for 'other people' use it as an example of questionable unorthodoxy in our domestic scene. A Valley Authority on the sacred Jordan River as a useful device for international cooperation is espoused by the same government officials who refer to its prototype at home as 'creeping socialism'; an asp in the bosom at home, a dove of peace abroad."

Whatever the judgment on TVA, one thing remains certain—its work is far from finished. New times bring new challenges. And as with any human endeavor, there are some effects that are not boons pure and simple, but pose new and thought-provoking problems. The conservation task for which TVA was created must go forward without faltering, for life does not stand still and no battle remains forever won. As Walt Whitman put it, "Now mark me well—it is provided in the essence of things that from any fruition of success, no matter what, shall come forth something to make a greater struggle necessary."

What are the greater struggles that face the valley today, after its initial "fruition of success?" Let us first consider the effects of the tremendous new power potential in the region.

From the outset industries were drawn to the valley, among other reasons because of its cheap and plentiful electricity. Electrometallurgical and electrochemical companies and pulp-making, paper-processing, and canning industries came. And then, starting with World War II, TVA was put under unusual pressure to produce more and more power to take care of the nation's military involvements. TVA's dam and power-plant construction were stepped up to provide for national defense, one of the purposes for which the authority had originally been created. Atomic plants were built at Oak Ridge, Tennessee, and Paducah, Kentucky. An Air Force wind-tunnel research center came to Tullahoma, Tennessee, and the NASA Marshall Space Flight Center to Huntsville, Alabama. By the early 1950s, the demand for electric power in the region—which had only had abundant electricity for some 15 years—was so great that the river's water power had to be gradually augmented by the use of more and more steam power.

Steam requires fuel for boilers, and in the 1950s TVA

had to look to the coal industry for large new supplies. Hopefully, the price would be low, for the cheaper the fuel, the cheaper could be the electricity.

At about this time, gigantic new earth-moving equipment came into use, and coal companies could engage in low-cost strip mining on an entirely new scale. By substituting powerful machinery for the old method of hand labor by miners, the size of the operations in the bituminous fields of Appalachia, for instance, soon became colossal.

What is strip mining, and why should conservationists be concerned about it? Harry M. Caudill, a native of the Cumberland Plateau in eastern Kentucky, saw it begin in the low hills and eventually move up the mountainside. He wrote in *Night Comes to the Cumberlands*:

The evil effects of open-cut mining are fantastically magnified when practiced in the mountains. Masses of shattered stone, shale, slate and dirt are cast pell-mell down the hillside. The first to go are the thin remaining layer of fertile topsoil and such trees as still find sustenance in it. The uprooted trees are flung down the slopes by the first cut. Then follows the sterile subsoil, shattered stone and slate. As the cut extends deeper into the hillside the process is repeated again and again . . .

Strip mining occurs largely in dry weather . . . During the hot season the nearby creek takes on a sallow hue after even the slightest shower. People living along its banks watch apprehensively . . .

Then come the rains of autumn and the freezes and thaws of winter. The descending water flays the loose

rubble, carrying thousands of tons of it into the streams
and onto the bottoms. The watery scalpel shaves inches
from the surface in almost instantaneous sheet erosion.
At the same time it carves gullies which deepen until the
streams reach the undisturbed soil far beneath . . .

What happened to the streams and rivers after this
general holocaust is told in this folk song of the 1960s:

Black Waters

I come from the moun-tains, Ken-tuck-y's my home, ___ Where the wild deer and the black bear so late-ly did roam; ___ By cool rush-ing wa-ter-falls the wild-flow-ers dream, ___ And ___ through ev-'ry green val-ley there runs a clear stream. ___ Now there's scenes of de-struc-tion on ev-'ry hand, ___ And there's

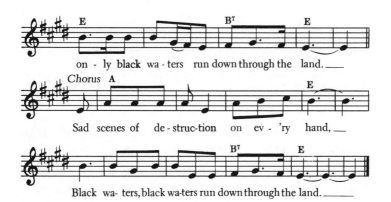

on - ly black wa - ters run down through the land. ___

Chorus A

Sad scenes of de - struc-tion on ev - 'ry hand, __

Black wa- ters, black wa-ters run down through the land. _____

O the quail, she's a pretty bird, she sings a sweet tongue,
In the roots of tall timbers she nests with her young;
But the hillside explodes with the dynamite's roar,
And the voices of the small birds will sound there no more,
And the hillside come a-sliding so awful and grand,
And the flooding black waters rise over my land.

CHORUS

In the rising of the springtime we planted our corn,
In the ending of the springtime we buried a son,
In summer came a nice man, says, Everything's fine—
My employer just requires a way to his mine.
Then they threw down my mountain and covered my corn,
And the grave on the hillside's a mile deeper down,

CHORUS:
And the man stands and talks with his hat in his hand
As the poisonous water spreads over my land.

Well I ain't got no money and not much of a home,
I own my own land—but my land's not my own.
But if I had ten million, somewheres thereabouts,
I would buy Perry County and I'd run 'em all out—
Sit down on the bank with my bait in my can,
And just watch the clear waters run down through my land.

CHORUS:
Well, wouldn't that be like the old Promised Land?
Black waters, black waters no more in my land!

© 1968 by Geordie Music Publishing, Inc. Used by permission of Warner Bros.–Seven Arts Music.

TVA was by no means the only purchaser of strip-mined coal. More than 80 percent of the coal in the five-state mining area went to private buyers such as US Coal and Coke. And in none of these states were there laws for the reclamation of the land.

TVA felt strongly that reclamation would be effective only if the individual states passed laws to enforce it, and so the authority's efforts were centered on legislation. But legislation is a slow process, and the work of the giant bulldozers and mammoth scoops was fast. It wasn't too long before strip mining in Appalachia attracted wide attention and created a furor.

Founded on conservation principles, TVA gradually awoke to its immediate responsibility. Since reclamation laws are still not adequate (though all the states but Alabama now have them) today the authority will buy only from surface-mine coal operators who include land reclamation clauses in their contracts. These provide for the control of water during the mining to reduce possible washing and contamination of streams and rivers. After the mining, the disturbed areas are planted with trees or grasses to hold the soil and restore the mine area's productivity and natural beauty.

From the Huntsville *Times* comes this description of what is being done:

*This was a beautiful wooded slope before
strip mining began in mountainous Appalachia.*

Strip-mining for coal in the mountains of northeast Alabama is not the often repeated story of miners intimidating property owners, ripping up valuable land and simply leaving it spoiled for future generations. The Farco Company mines 50,000 tons of coal a month from Sand Mountain and speeds all of it, via truck and barge, to TVA's nearby Widows Creek Steam Plant. While its mammoth machinery is chewing at another tract of sandy, rocky terrain, school boys are setting pine seedlings with a hand tool and a helicopter is strewing treated pine seeds over the bared rock piles.

But can all or even most of the livid scars inflicted on the earth by strip mining, especially on steep mountainous slopes, ever truly be healed? One wonders.

Other possible areas of greater struggle for the valley are emerging out of the technological advances that have been introduced there. Thus, as the atomic reactor begins to compete with coal for power production (and TVA is already entering the atomic era), many predictable and perhaps some unpredictable problems loom ahead. A known concern is the safe disposal of atomic wastes; another is the handling of "thermal pollution" produced when cooling waters are returned at elevated temperatures into streams and lakes. This kind of contamination has sometimes proved devastating to aquatic life. And even the new fertilizers and pesticides, washed off the land by rainfall, are sometimes culprits and need further investigation.

In addition, careless use or overuse of newly developed resources may seriously endanger them. Instances are at hand: harnessing the Tennessee River has created an abundant supply of good water for cities and industries, but as urbanization and manufacturing increase, the problem of waste disposal also increases. New and intensive programs will be needed to stem the existing and potential tides of pollution. Similarly, when the TVA reservoirs transformed muddy streams into clear lakes, fish multiplied, but so too did fishermen, canoers, and picnickers. Recreation means people, and so many have been attracted to the waters that the pollution from pleasure craft has become an irksome problem.

The handwriting on the wall says, in substance, "In using his river man can, in turn, narrow its usefulness." And the same can be said of the valley's "excellent canopy, the sky," which becomes less and less excellent when it begins to serve as an upside-down aerial garbage can. These and other problems—problems relating not only to water quality but to air pollution as well—are part of the active research of today and tomorrow going on in the laboratories of TVA.

But such environmental threats confront not only the Tennessee valley but every region in the nation. Barry Commoner, professor of plant physiology at Washington University, generalized about the problems modern technology poses:

In the eager search for the benefits of modern science and technology we have become enticed into a nearly fatal illusion: that we have at last escaped from the dependence of man on the balance of nature. The truth is tragically different. We have become not less dependent on the balance of nature but more dependent on it. Modern technology has so stressed the web of processes in the living environment at its most vulnerable points that there is little leeway left in the system. I believe that unless we begin to match our technological power with a deeper understanding of the balance of nature we run the risk of destroying this planet as a suitable place for human habitation.

The same concern was expressed somewhat differently by Aubrey J. Wagner, present chairman of TVA's board:

Our situation has aptly been compared with the astronauts in their orbiting capsules. They can survive only so long as their resources on the capsule—food and water, air, and equipment—hold out; and only so long as they are not overwhelmed by their own wastes.

The earth itself, of course, is but a large orbiting capsule. Its inhabitants—you and I—will survive only so long as we can make the resources we have aboard feed and clothe us; and only so long as we are not overwhelmed by the growing cascades of our own wastes.

But surely we seek more than survival. . . . I think we all seek the kind of environment—cultural as well as physical—in which every man is equally free to develop his skills and talents, to achieve his goals, to experience a sense of accomplishment and personal fulfillment.

To reach toward such a goal for *all* people, we must examine still another area of the greater struggle—the migration of the dispossessed—the uneducated, the unskilled—away from the Tennessee valley where certain kinds of labor are no longer needed. Historically the valley has had more people than it could employ, and this resulted in two migrations: one from the farm to nearby cities, and another to cities in the industrial North, where job opportunities were supposedly greater. As new industries came to the valley, both kinds of migration diminished, and today there is even a small net inmigration.

Still, a number of people leave the valley every year to seek menial or nonexistent employment elsewhere, and the effects of this outmigration accumulate when added to the streams of people leaving other rural regions for the cities. Particularly is it true of Negroes and poor whites from the hills that they usually have no choice but to be herded into urban ghettos. Thus changes in rural America reach out into the crowded complexity of decaying inner cities hundreds of miles away.

In a book called *In the Midst of Plenty*, journalist Ben H. Bagdikian gives this description of the outmigration of people no longer able to scratch a living from the land:

Into the cities they pour, refugees from a silent revolution.

In Chicago the white folk from the countryside come mostly by Trailways bus, carrying all they own; a suitcase tied with rope, an old trunk, three shopping bags, a folded baby buggy, a bag of grits, clutching a letter from a relative come earlier with an address and a warning, "Don't take the cabs, they'll cheat you."

If they are colored they come mostly by the great iron

artery in Southern Negro life, the Illinois Central Railroad, getting off in awe under the largest building they ever saw, carrying their old suitcases and trunks, cardboard boxes with clothes and pans . . .

In a city as big as Chicago the newcomers face a strange new world. Old courage is not enough, previous skills meaningless, and what may have been minor disadvantages in education or family cohesion suddenly become catastrophic . . .

But it is not just Chicago. It is the same in New York, Los Angeles, Philadelphia, Detroit, Cleveland, Washington, St. Louis—all the great cities.

Can or should the people in the Tennessee valley do anything about the problems of megalopolis? Indirectly, they are. By taking an active part in improving conditions in their own region—particularly in the fast urbanizing sections—they and TVA are helping to ease the problems of big cities far away. When people have a genuine choice about staying or leaving, when others are attracted to the valley because there are good jobs and because the living is good, pressure on the ghettos begins to lessen, even if just a little.

In 1967 a Washington *Post* staff writer offered these comments along with several interesting suggestions:

Riding his horse through Washington's Rock Creek Park 60 years ago, Gifford Pinchot had an inspiration. And that has a great deal to do with all the new jobs in Decatur, Alabama, and with city children who will go to school for a week in the beautiful woods of Land Between the

Lakes next summer and watch deer emerge as dusk approaches. . . .

But now that TVA has proven its success as the world's foremost experiment in regional economic planning and development (with wonderful new recreation parks thrown in as a bonus), it would seem logical to carry Pinchot's idea even further and pioneer the physical development—the regional planning and building of more attractive cities and "new towns" and new transportation techniques that are now so much talked about.

Working with the states and communities in its valley, and with the support of the federal government, TVA could be the first agency in the nation to avert urban pollution and plan comprehensively for urban growth . . . for a well-planned urban environment is obviously the next phase in attacking Pinchot's "one central problem of the use of the earth for the good of man."

The more we become aware of the interrelatedness of our rural and urban problems, the more it becomes evident that no spot on earth can be considered an "ilande unto itself," no matter how far it has progressed in the solution of its own problems. We must not draw the limits of any area too tightly, for each part of the earth is in truth a "part of the maine."

The Gifford Pinchots and George Norrises of today —those moved as these men were by the conservation idea—will not be surprised to find their concerns turning increasingly to urban fronts. In Norris' era, conservationists looked after the four great renewable resources —soil, water, forests, and wildlife—but today the movement cannot remain so limited. It must reach out to encompass the total environment—urban as well as rural, manmade as well as natural.

At its inception TVA was an innovator—in planning, in technology, in resource use. Today further innovations are needed, and certainly some are already in the making: creative planning for the valley's larger cities to meet the challenge of the new inmigration; creative planning for its small towns and cities so that outmigration becomes a choice, not a necessity. The vision of the people in the valley must remain clear and must be coupled with foresight to cope intelligently with our fast-growing technology, and with understanding to maintain that balance of nature on which our very lives depend.

Finally, how are we to assess the worth of planned resource development? David Lilienthal gave us a clue as early as 1943 in an entry in his *Journal*:

To the extent that it removes the abject degradation of hunger and cold and fear of these things; to the extent that it removes the despoiling and exhaustion of natural resources, the pollution of streams and laying waste of forests it is certainly good. But beyond this no one can say with any assurance.

What these technical developments will mean in terms of the values of human life—kindness, charity, truthfulness, etc.—is what will determine the final answer: is it good or not.

Much has happened in the Tennessee valley since Lilienthal wrote these lines, much that is good. Nevertheless, the final answer cannot be given, for it continues to depend on people, on the manner in which they stretch their minds and hearts, and on the decisions they make today and in the days to come.

One Man's Hands

One man's hands can't break a pris-on down,—
— Two men's hands can't break a pris-on down,——
But if two and two and fif-ty make a mil-lion, We'll see that day come 'round, We'll see that day come 'round.——

One man's feet can't walk around the land,
Two men's feet can't walk around the land,
But if two and two and fifty make a million,

CHORUS:
We'll see that day come 'round,
We'll see that day come 'round.

One man's strength can't break the color bar,
Two men's strength can't break the color bar,
But if two and two and fifty make a million,

CHORUS:
We'll see that day come 'round,
We'll see that day come 'round.

One man's eyes can't see the way ahead,
Two men's eyes can't see the way ahead,
But if two and two and fifty make a million,

CHORUS:
We'll see that day come 'round,
We'll see that day come 'round.

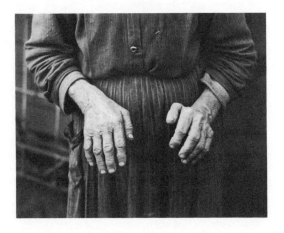

BIBLIOGRAPHY

Maps and Map Guides

One of the best ways of learning about TVA is to visit the Tennessee region and explore for yourself. Go and hike through the forests and on the mountain trails, and explore the lakes, dams, and tributary streams by boat and canoe. Unless otherwise indicated, the various maps and guides mentioned below may be procured by writing to:

> Tennessee Valley Authority
> Map Information and Records Unit
> 110 Pound Building
> Chattanooga, Tennessee 37401

Topographical maps: The fundamental map sources for canoer, walker, or cyclist are the topographic quadrangle maps of the United States Geological Survey, available in various scales. Maps for the Tennessee River region are indexed on *Index to TVA-USGS Topographic Maps*. This sheet, which is free, is indispensable as a guide to the region and the maps you will need in order to explore any portion of it.

Recreation maps: The Tennessee Valley Authority has also made some fine recreation maps covering the entire span of the Tennessee River and principal tributaries. The key to these maps, also free, which will tell you at a glance which ones you may need, is *Recreation Maps—Tennessee Valley Lakes.* The maps themselves show roads, dams, public parks, wildlife areas, boat-launching sites, and other facilities. They are specially designed for use by people who wish to explore the lakes and dams and the countryside immediately adjoining these. The price for each map is nominal—from ten to twenty-five cents. Also helpful is a general map folder and guide entitled *Recreation on TVA Lakes.*

Navigation charts: The Tennessee lakes can also be explored by motorboat. Here you will need the *Index to Navigation Charts and Maps.* Individual charts cost fifty cents, a complete folio for the entire river system, ten dollars.

Guide to tributary streams: For white-water canoeing, TVA recommends the tributary streams, while the lakes offer pleasant but quieter waters. Regarding either, you will need a small-scale map entitled *Tennessee Recreational Waters,* issued by the State of Tennessee Game and Fish Commission. Another good booklet is *Folbot Holidays,* providing information about canoeing streams, type of water, difficulty of navigation, and surrounding scenery. This is available for one dollar by writing to the Folbot Corporation, Charleston, South Carolina.

History

For the early history of the valley, and especially a picture of its luxuriant wildlife before pioneer settlement, there is now available a modern edition of the original *William Bartram, Travels,* New York: Dover Publications, Inc., 1958. The most comprehensive overall history, still in print, is Donald Davidson's *The Tennessee* in two volumes: *The Old River: Frontier to Secession* and *The New River: Civil War to TVA,* New York: Holt, Rinehart and Winston, Inc.,

---

* Indicates a paperback edition.

1946 and 1948 respectively. A much briefer historical treatment, but a quite original one because each of its chapters is followed by a guide to possible field trips, is *William T. Alderson, *Tennessee: A Students' Guide to Localized History*, New York: Teachers College Press, Columbia University, 1966.

The hard way of life of some of the people of the southeastern region of our country is conveyed in the following two very human and moving books whose settings neighbor the Tennessee valley. For the plight of the sharecroppers during the great depression, see *James Agee and Walker Evans, *Let Us Now Praise Famous Men*, New York: Ballantine Books, Inc., 1966. And for the traditions and tenacity of the hill folk, see *Jesse Stuart, *The Thread That Runs So True*, New York: Charles Scribner's Sons, 1958.

There are several good accounts of the coming of TVA and its varied impact. The classic treatment, written in 1943, is *David Lilienthal, *TVA: Democracy on the March*, Chicago: Quadrangle Books, Inc., 1966. The whole inside story is told at more length in volume one of Lilienthal's *Journal: TVA Years 1939–1945*, New York: Harper & Row, Publishers, 1964. For politics, *Arthur M. Schlesinger, Jr., *The Coming of the New Deal* (vol. 2 of *The Age of Roosevelt*), Boston: Houghton Mifflin Company (Sentry), 1965, has some very informative pages. James Agee's insightful articles on TVA, originally written for *Fortune* magazine, are excerpted at somewhat greater length than I have done in *Frank Freidel, ed., *The New Deal and the American People*, Englewood Cliffs: Prentice-Hall, Inc., 1964. A warmly human picture of the "Father of TVA," George Norris, is in *Fighting Liberal: The Autobiography of George W. Norris*, New York: P. F. Collier, Inc., 1961. Finally, anyone who wishes to know the many phases of TVA's activities may write for *A *Bibliography for the* TVA *Program*, Knoxville: TVA, 1966.

Conservation

There are a number of classics on the subject of conservation, and many new titles are now appearing in paperback. Two of the former are George Marsh, *Man and Nature*, Boston: Harvard University Press, 1965, originally published in 1865; and Gifford Pinchot, *Fight for Conservation*, Seattle: University of Washington Press, 1910. Both are currently in print.

Newer titles that I especially recommend are: *John Storer, *The Web of Life*, New York: Signet Books, 1953; and Paul B. Sears, *Living Landscape*, New York: Basic Books, Inc., Publishers, 1966. The very disturbing portrait on strip mining from which I have drawn is *Harry M. Caudill, *Night Comes to the Cumberlands: A Biography of a Depressed Area*, Boston: Little, Brown and Company (Atlantic Monthly Press), 1963.

Songs

A large general collection is *J. H. Cox, *Folk Songs of the South*, New York: Oak Publications, Inc., 1963. My own favorite, a book out of print but available at many libraries, is D. Scarborough, *A Song Catcher in the Southern Mountains*, New York: Columbia University Press, 1937. For songs about the depression years, a handsome (though expensive) hardcover anthology is *A. Lomax and others, eds., *Hard Hitting Songs for Hard-hit People*, New York: Oak Publications, Inc., 1968. Jean Ritchie, the composer of "Black Waters," has had published a song collection which also includes reminiscences about the life of a young girl in the Kentucky hills. It is *Singing Family of the Cumberlands*, New York: Oak Publications, Inc., 1963.

ACKNOWLEDGMENTS

The words "thank you" are pallid conveyors of feeling, yet they will have to serve as best they can. Since this is a living history, thanks go to all the authors whose written words give life and color to the narrative. I am especially grateful to the Conservation Foundation for making possible the writing of this book; and to the staff of TVA for giving me every possible assistance. TVA staff members dug up rich material and also read the finished chapters, but only after making it clear that accuracy of fact was the only aspect they would judge. An oft-repeated thank you goes to my friend Dr. Nancy Ziebur for her thoughtful, perceptive suggestions. And a round of thanks to Harriet Bennett and Edna Gengerke who worked so hard to bring forth a clean copy from the chaos of my scrawled-over scrawl. Finally, to my editors, and most particularly to Judy Engelhardt, thank you for helping to make this book a reality.

Grateful acknowledgment is made to the following for permission to reprint from their works:

Alfred A. Knopf, Inc. for *The Valley and Its People*, by R. L. Duffus.

Beacon Press for *In the Midst of Plenty*, by Ben H. Bagdikian. Copyright © 1964 by Ben H. Bagdikian.

Charles Scribner's Sons for *The Thread That Runs So True*, by Jesse Stuart. Copyright 1949 by Jesse Stuart.

Chilton Book Company for *There's Laughter in the Air*, edited by Jack Gaver and David Dachs. Copyright 1945.

Crowell Collier and Macmillan, Inc. for material from "Collier's Weekly," June 1934.

Harper & Row, Publishers for *The Journals of David E. Lilienthal: Volume I: The TVA Years*. Copyright © 1964 by David E. Lilienthal.

Holt, Rinehart and Winston, Inc. for *The Tennessee, Volume II*, by Donald Davidson. Copyright 1948 by Donald Davidson.

Houghton Mifflin Company for *Let Us Now Praise Famous Men*, by James Agee and Walker Evans.

Little, Brown and Company for *Night Comes to the Cumberlands*, by Harry M. Caudill. Copyright © 1962, 1963 by Harry M. Caudill.

McGraw-Hill Book Company for *America Begins Again*, by Katharine Glover. Copyright 1939 by McGraw-Hill Book Company.

The New York Times Company for portions of two articles. Copyright 1927/30.

The University of North Carolina Press for an article by Bruce Crawford in *Culture of the South*, edited by W. T. Couch. For *These Are Our Lives*, by the Federal Writer's Project of the WPA.

Yale University Press for *Travels: 1958*, by William Bartram.

Grateful acknowledgment is made for the use of illustrations:

Arthur Tress, 76, 161, 177; *Book of Trees* by William C. Grimm, 153; Brown Brothers, Inc., 55; Chicago *Tribune*, 138; Library of Congress, Farm Security Administration, 32, 126, 187; Memphis *Press-Scimitar*, 141; New-York Historical Society, 16; New York Public Library, 24; Tennessee Valley Authority, frontispiece, 29, 43, 48, 50, 64, 73, 81, 87, 92, 97, 106, 110, 113, 117, 135, 158, 177, 183; Washington *Evening Star*, 66; Yale University Art Gallery, 11. The jacket photograph—from TVA—shows a meeting of construction workers at Douglas Dam, October 6, 1942.

INDEX

MARTHA MUNZER's professional interests have for many years been science and the conservation movement, while personally she describes herself as "living in the four seasons." Much of her book, in fact, was written out-of-doors, off Long Island Sound near Mamaroneck, New York, where she lives.

Mrs. Munzer was among the first women graduates of MIT and subsequently taught chemistry at the Fieldston School in New York for twenty-five years. In 1954 she resigned to join the Conservation Foundation, and currently she also lectures and works with young people at the Wave Hill Center for Environmental Studies in Riverdale, New York. Her other books include *Pockets of Hope* and *Planning Our Town*.

JOHN ANTHONY SCOTT has taught at Columbia and Amherst Colleges, and since 1951 has been chairman of the Department of History at the Fieldston School, New York. He is currently a Professor of Legal History at Rutgers University. Among the books he has authored or edited are *The Ballad of America* and *The Diary of the American Revolution*.

The text of this book is set in a type face called Electra.
Composed and bound by The Book Press, Brattleboro, Vt.
Printed by Halliday Lithograph Corp., West Hanover, Mass.
Typography by Atha Tehon